Discover
Britain's
historic
houses

Middle England

Discover Britain's

Published by Reader's Digest Association Ltd
London • New York • Sydney • Montreal

Reader's Digest

historic houses
Middle England

Simon Jenkins

Contents

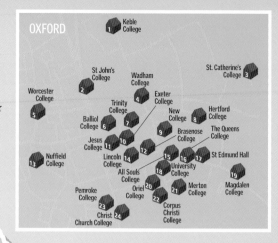

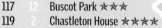

The best in Britain

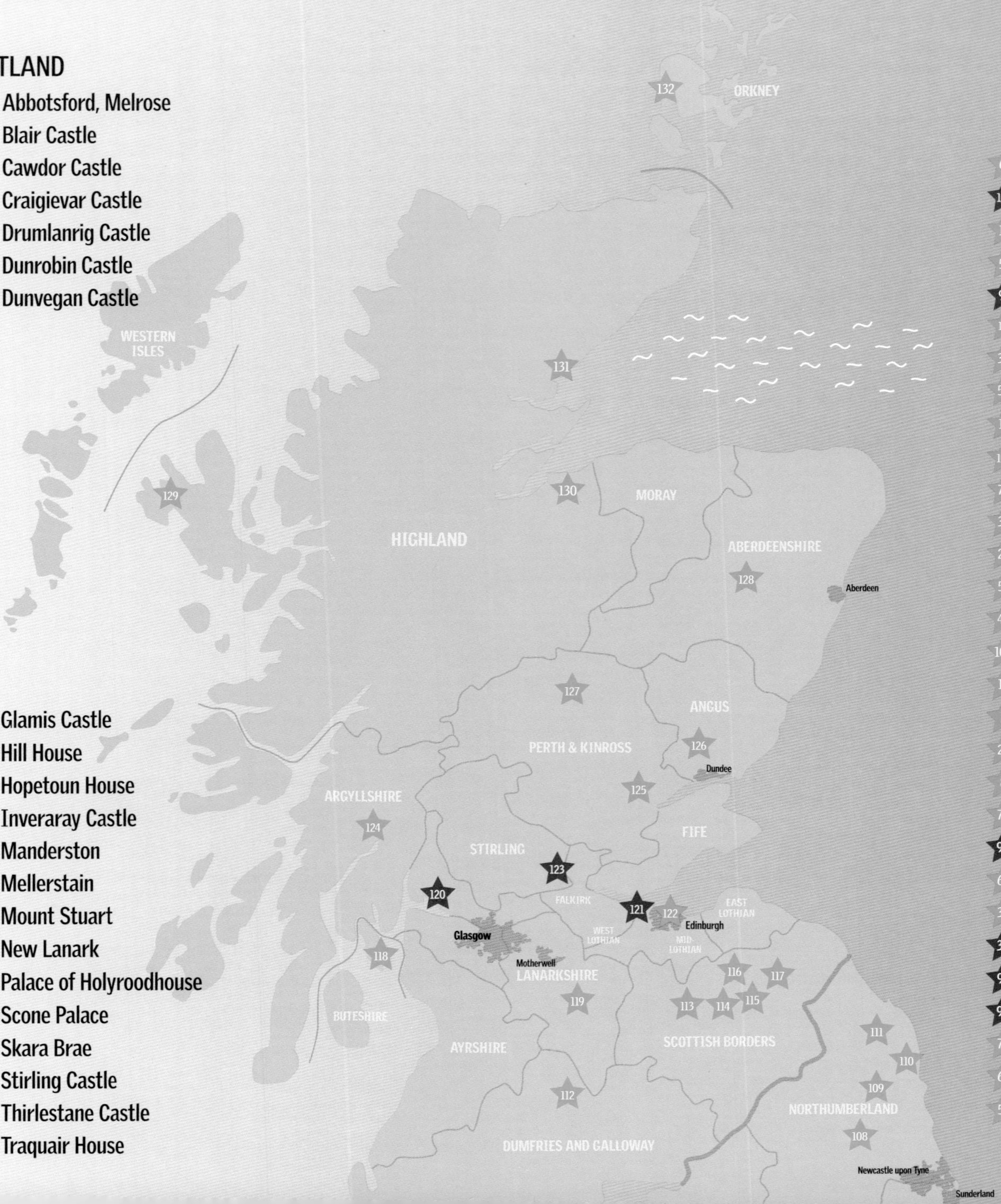
ORKNEY
WESTERN ISLES
HIGHLAND
MORAY
ABERDEENSHIRE
Aberdeen
ANGUS
Dundee
PERTH & KINROSS
ARGYLLSHIRE
FIFE
STIRLING
FALKIRK
WEST LOTHIAN
EAST LOTHIAN
MID-LOTHIAN
Edinburgh
Glasgow
Motherwell
LANARKSHIRE
BUTESHIRE
AYRSHIRE
SCOTTISH BORDERS
NORTHUMBERLAND
DUMFRIES AND GALLOWAY
Newcastle upon Tyne
Sunderland
132
131
129
130
128
127
126
125
124
123
120
121
122
118
119
116
117
113
114
115
111
110
109
108
112

SCOTLAND

- 114 Abbotsford, Melrose
- 127 Blair Castle
- 130 Cawdor Castle
- 128 Craigievar Castle
- 112 Drumlanrig Castle
- 131 Dunrobin Castle
- 129 Dunvegan Castle
- 126 Glamis Castle
- 120 Hill House
- 121 Hopetoun House
- 124 Inveraray Castle
- 117 Manderston
- 115 Mellerstain
- 118 Mount Stuart
- 119 New Lanark
- 122 Palace of Holyroodhouse
- 125 Scone Palace
- 132 Skara Brae
- 123 Stirling Castle
- 116 Thirlestane Castle
- 113 Traquair House

- 61 Canons Ashby
- 102 Castle Howard
- 14 Charleston
- 54 Chastleton House *
- 91 Chatsworth House
- 111 Chillingham Castle
- 36 Chiswick House
- 56 Claydon House *
- 16 Cothay Manor
- 109 Cragside
- 70 Deene Park
- 38 Dennis Severs House
- 28 Dyrham Park
- 52 Eastnor Castle
- 40 Eltham Palace
- 100 Fairfax House
- 13 Firle Place
- 3 Forde Abbey
- 27 Godinton Park
- 8 Goodwood House
- 78 Grimsthorpe Castle
- 90 Haddon Hall
- 66 Hagley Hall
- 35 Ham House
- 34 Hampton Court
- 93 Hardwick Hall
- 98 Harewood House
- 76 Harlaxton Manor
- 65 Harvington Hall
- 51 Hatfield House *
- 22 Hever Castle
- 80 Holkham Hall
- 37 Home House
- 79 Houghton Hall
- 107 Hutton-in-the-Forest
- 25 Ightham Mote
- 74 Kedleston Hall
- 21 Kensington Palace
- 5 Kingston Lacy
- 50 Knebworth House *
- 24 Knole
- 29 Lacock Abbey
- 1 Lanhydrock
- 26 Leeds Castle
- 104 Levens Hall
- 19 Longleat
- 89 Lyme Park
- 53 Madresfield Court
- 48 Magdalen College *
- 17 Montacute House
- 101 Newby Hall
- 94 Newstead Abbey
- 96 Nostell Priory
- 6 Osborne House
- 32 Osterley Park
- 72 Oxburgh Hall
- 10 Parham House
- 23 Penshurst Place
- 9 Petworth House
- 106 Raby Castle
- 59 Ragley Hall
- 41 Restoration House

WALES

84 Beaumaris Castle
82 Caernarfon Castle *
43 Caerphilly Castle
42 Castell Coch
86 Conwy Castle *
87 Erddig *
85 Plas Mawr
83 Plas Newydd
73 Powis Castle
45 Raglan Castle
44 Tredegar House

ENGLAND

110 Alnwick Castle
62 Althorp
68 Arbury Hall
11 Arundel Castle
95 Astley Hall
4 Athelhampton House
58 Audley End
15 Bateman's
77 Belton House
75 Belvoir Castle
99 Beningbrough Hall
46 Berkeley Castle *
47 Blenheim Palace *
81 Blickling Hall
92 Bolsover Castle
69 Boughton House
12 Brighton Pavilion *
55 Broughton Castle *
71 Burghley House
103 Burton Agnes Hall
97 Burton Constable Hall

2 Saltram House
18 Sherborne Castle
105 Sizergh Castle
88 Speke Hall
39 Spencer House
63 St John's College
33 Syon House *
30 The Vyne
64 Trinity College
7 Uppark
49 Waddesdon Manor *

108 Wallington Hall
60 Warwick Castle
67 Wightwick Manor
20 Wilton House *
31 Windsor Castle *
57 Woburn Abbey *

5 Star
4 Star
* Featured in this book

I visited these buildings after writing a book on English churches and the experience was as moving as it was different. While places of worship were built according to the authority and liturgy of the Church, people built houses for themselves. A house was useful first and beautiful second, and from this derives the joy of visiting houses. They are a conversation between utility and beauty down the ages.

In defining the word 'house' I soon found that I could not sensibly distinguish castle from palace, house from hut, roof from ruin. My list embraces any structure in which men and women have laid their heads, provided that they are in some degree accessible to public view. The selection is a personal list and the commentary is a personal vision, warts and all.

Simon Jenkins

Historic houses
of Middle England

Poor, rich little **Bedfordshire**. With the exception of Henry Flitcroft's palace for the Duke of Bedford at Woburn, the county is bereft of great houses. Bushmead is a modest survivor of the Middle Ages; Houghton a ruined exemplar of the Elizabethan Renaissance. Wrest Park, with a Thomas Archer pavilion in its formal garden, offers only a ghost of the eccentric Earl de Grey. Old Warden has a charming Swiss cottage in its grounds. My most unexpected find was the recreation of the bedroom of the colourful Victorian medievalist, William Burges inthe Cecil Higgins house in Bedford.

Buckinghamshire guards London from the north and west, or perhaps guards the north and west from London and though its towns have been terribly abused, its country is well protected, as are its great houses.Of the pre-classical era Dorney still has its 15th-century hall, and Nether Winchendon and Chenies display Elizabethan remains. But it was the 18th

century that took Buckinghamshire by storm. Vanbrugh gave Stowe its entrance front, followed by Kent, Leoni, Adam and others. Chicheley has a scholarly exterior by Smith of Warwick. The Dashwoods brought the Grand Tour to life at West Wycombe. At Claydon, Lord Verney produced the most exciting Chinese Rococo rooms in England. Charles Barry's great house at Cliveden has been well restored. Disraeli adapted Hughenden as his country seat, and Burn rebuilt Taplow for the Grenfells. The Rothschilds chose French château-style at Waddesdon and neo-Tudor at Ascott.

Hertfordshire was ideal for aspiring 16th-century courtiers and City merchants with no landed estate and a need for a country house within a day's ride of London. This also applied to the monarch. Henry VIII kept his children out of harm's way at Hatfield Palace. This house passed to the Earls of Salisbury in the 17th century, who built next to it one of the great mansions of Jacobean England. Nearby lodged other Tudor dignitaries; Cardinal Wolsey at Moor Park, Lord Lytton at Knebworth, Lord Egerton at Ashridge and Nicholas Bacon at Gorhambury. Moor Park had a succession of aristocratic owners. Robert Taylor rebuilt Gorhambury for the Earl of Verulam, and James Paine Brocket Hall for Lord Melbourne. Ashridge was rebuilt in grandiloquent Gothic by the Wyatts for the Duke of Bridgewater. Knebworth was then decorated and fantasized by Bulwer-Lytton. In the 20th century, Shaw brought early socialism to Shaw's Corner and Parker and Unwin brought the same to Letchworth Garden City. Which did more to change the world is moot.

In addition to the architectual treasure house of Oxford, **Oxfordshire** is rich in early houses. The Middle Ages left Minster Lovell, Stanton Harcourt and the almshouses at Ewelme. The Elizabethans produced the splendid chambers of Broughton and the lovely Thamesside mansion of Mapledurham. Few English houses so typify the Jacobean era as Chastleton, its ancient furniture and tapestries frozen in time. After the Restoration, Lord Craven celebrated his love for the 'Winter Queen' at Ashdown. The 18th century began with Vanbrugh's great trumpet blast at Blenheim, later to be set in one of Capability Brown's most stylish parks. James Gibbs built Ditchley with interiors by Kent and Flitcroft. Kent also converted Rousham in the Gothick style. In the past two centuries, Kelmscott took the fancy of William Morris, while William Morris, maker of cars, left the county's most curious relic at Nuffield Place, filled with his inventive ingenuity.

The **City of Oxford** contains the most extensive group of medieval and pre-Georgian buildings in England. The earliest colleges, University, Merton and Balliol, all date from the arrival of scholars from Paris in 1229. The oldest collegiate buildings are those of Merton dating from 1304. After the Black Death money flowed into proper collegiate endowment, culminating in the three grandest benefactors, William of Wykeham (New), Henry Chichele (All Souls) and William Waynflete (Magdalen). All later foundations took New College as their model. The next burst of building took place after the Restoration, producing works by Hawksmoor, Wren and others. As at Cambridge, the Victorians reverted to Gothic and Tudor revivalism. Oxford, like Cambridge, suffered grievously from the university expansion of the 1970s and 1980s. The best modern buildings are the most recent, notably by Richard MacCormac at Worcester, Wadham and St John's.

★ STAR RATINGS AND ACCESSIBILITY ★★★★

The 'star' ratings are entirely my personal choice (but see note below). They rate the overall quality of the house as presented to the public, and not gardens or other attractions. On balance I scaled down houses, however famous, for not being easily accessible or for being only partly open.

The top rating, five stars, is given to those houses that qualify as 'international' celebrities. Four stars are awarded to houses of outstanding architectural quality and public display. Three-star houses comprise the run of good historic houses, well displayed and worthy of national promotion. Two and one-star houses are of more local interest, are hard to visit, or have just one significant feature.

Accessibility varies greatly, from buildings that are open all year to houses that can only be visited 'by appointment' (rarely, I have broken my rule and included a private property that is not open at all, but is viewable from nearby walks or public gardens). Opening hours tend to alter from year to year, but an indication of how accessible a house is to visitors is given at the start of each entry, together with brief information on location and ownership. Many of the houses are National Trust or English Heritage properties, some are now museums or hotels, others are privately owned by families who open to the public for part of the year (English Heritage grant requirements insist on 28 days minimum). Some owners may, understandably, seek to cluster visitors on particular days. More details for each house are given at the back of this book, and readers are advised to check before visiting.

A final note, houses are, or should be, living things subject to constant change and how we view them is bound to be a subject of debate. I welcome any correction or comment, especially from house owners, sent to me c/o the publisher.

NOTE: On the UK map (pages 6-7) the 4 and 5-star houses in England and Wales were selected by Simon Jenkins. Those in Scotland were selected by Hamish Scott and the editors of Reader's Digest.

Architectural timeline
and Middle England houses in brief

Abingdon: Long Alley Almshouses
Almshouses run around three sides of the churchyard at Abingdon. Long Alley, originally founded in 1446 and still in occupation.

Abingdon: Merchant's House
A medieval hall house with fine original decoration. Now two houses with 'bridge' between, created when a carriageway was created on the ground floor in the 19th century.

All Souls College
College of fellows, founded 1438. The Great Quad, was designed by Hawksmoor in Gothick style to compliment the medieval front quad.

Ardington
Georgian house built for the Baring family in 1720 in an English Baroque style. Inside is a double staircase and panelled dining room.

Ascott House
English cottage style on a grand scale, a mock-Tudor weekend hunting lodge built for the Rothschilds in the 1870s. Home to some fine works of art.

Ashdown House
A Restoration mansion built for Charles I's sister, Elizabeth, known as the 'Winter Queen'. A neat, square house with steep-pitched roof, flanked by two matching pavilions.

Ashridge
Begun in 1809 by James Wyatt and finished by his nephew Sir Jeffry Wyatville. A Gothick mansion, complete with hammerbeam roof in the medieval-style entrance hall.

Balliol College
College founded in 1282 and rebuilt in the 19th century by William Butterfield and Alfred Waterhouse in Gothic Revival style.

Bedford: Castle Close
An early Victorian villa with late Victorian, recreated interiors; now a museum. Features a bedroom completely furnished with William Burges pieces.

Blenheim Palace
A true palace, designed by Sir John Vanbrugh with Nicholas Hawksmoor, and intended as a reward for the Duke of Marlborough after his victory at the Battle of Blenheim in 1704.

Bletchley Park
A late-Victorian mansion with elements of Dutch, Tudor, Elizabethan and Jacobean architecture; home to the Enigma code breakers.

Boarstall Tower
Part of a house with origins in the 11th century. What remains is a medieval gatehouse that became used as a banqueting house at the end of the 16th century.

Brasenose College
A Tudor college founded in 1509; its Old Quad is of the same date. Its chapel uses medieval elements but dates from the mid-17th century.

Brocket Hall
A Georgian house by James Paine, begun in 1760. Paine's interiors have survived; the saloon is decorated in an Adam style.

Broughton Castle
Medieval manor, dating from the 1300s and once home to William of Wykeham, that was 'modernized' in the 16th century. Inside are magnificent plasterwork and panelling.

Buscot Old Parsonage
William-and-Mary style house, built in 1701. The steep hipped roof is faced with Cotswold stone tiles; the front steps are Baroque.

Buscot Park
A Georgian house of the 1780s, owned by a 19th-century art collector who transformed the saloon as a setting for paintings by Edward Burne-Jones.

Bushmead Priory
The remains of an Augustinian priory. The refectory and a two-storey wing can still be seen, with surviving wall paintings and medieval window tracery.

Chalfont St Giles: Milton's Cottage
A small 16th-century cottage, home to the poet John Milton who moved to Chalfont St Giles in 1665. The rooms he inhabited are preserved.

Chastleton House
A 17th-century Cotswold mansion built to a design that was old fashioned then, and is little altered today. The Jacobean style and atmosphere of the house are preserved intact.

Chenies Manor
Medieval hall house extended and altered by the Bedfords when it came into their hands in the 16th century. Fine Tudor interiors survive.

Chiltern Open Air Museum
Collection of vernacular buildings, reconstructed in a rural spot; they include a post-war prefab, an 18th-century toll house and two cottages converted from an 18th-century barn.

Chilton House
A Queen-Anne style mansion built in the 1740s in the Vale of Aylesbury. Fine 18th-century plasterwork remains in the interior rooms.

Christ Church College
Founded in 1527 by Cardinal Wolsey. The Tom Tower is one of Oxford's landmarks; started by Wolsey, it was finished by Christopher Wren in a style he felt appropriate.

Claydon House
Remaining wing of a once-palatial mid-Georgian house. The interior decoration by carver Luke Lightfoot is a sublime example of Rococo style.

Cliveden
A grandiose mansion in Italian style, high on a bluff overlooking the Thames. Designed by Sir Charles Barry who incorporated wings of an earlier house, by Thomas Archer.

Cogges Manor
A manorial farmhouse, dating back to the Middle Ages, now maintained as it would have been in the 19th century, furnished in typical Victorian style.

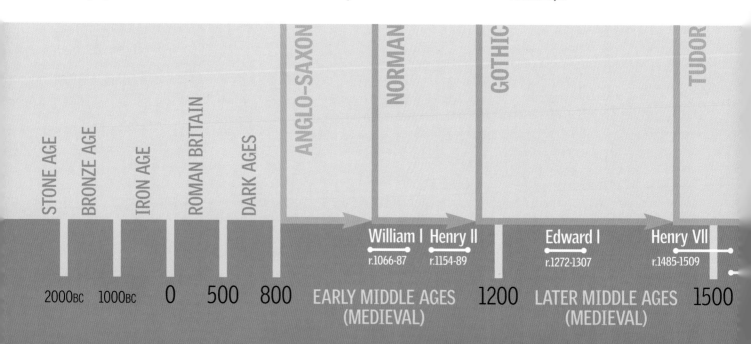

STONE AGE BRONZE AGE IRON AGE ROMAN BRITAIN DARK AGES ANGLO-SAXON NORMAN GOTHIC TUDOR

William I r.1066-87 Henry II r.1154-89 Edward I r.1272-1307 Henry VII r.1485-1509

2000BC 1000BC 0 500 800 EARLY MIDDLE AGES (MEDIEVAL) 1200 LATER MIDDLE AGES (MEDIEVAL) 1500

Corpus Christi College
A Tudor college, founded in 1517, with a Jacobean library. Georgian buildings were added in the early 18th century and the Great Hall was updated.

Ditchley Park
Restrained Georgian mansion, built in 1720–26 by Francis Smith of Warwick; his work was later altered by James Gibbs, with further additions by William Kent and Henry Flitcroft

Dorney Court
A Tudor house that was given a Georgian facelift in the 1730s. This was replaced with a 'Tudor' façade in the 1900s; it is hard to distinguish what is original from what is new or imported.

Ewelme Almshouses
Red-brick almshouses dating from 1437 and still in use. They were built around a courtyard as part of a community enclave that combined church and school.

Exeter College
Founded in around 1314 for West-Country students, the college was mainly rebuilt in the early 17th century. The chapel was designed by Sir Gilbert Scott and is based on the Sainte Chapelle in Paris.

Fawley Court
A Restoration mansion on the banks of the Thames, the interiors were decorated by James Wyatt at the end of the 18th century. The double-cube saloon has a ceiling attributed to Grinling Gibbons.

Gorhambury
A Palladian house built in 1777, fronted with an impressive Corinthian portico. It replaced an earlier Tudor mansion; the ruins remain as a feature in the park.

Grey's Court
The remains of an Elizabethan mansion with a Georgian gothick extension by Henry Keene; part of a grouping around a courtyard with medieval and Tudor towers.

Hanbury Manor
A red-brick Jacobethan-style 'manor' house built in 1890 by the firm of Sir Ernest George & Peto. The interior decoration includes a number of Elizabethan and Renaissance motifs.

Garden cities

At the end of the 19th century, England's cities were overcrowded and the countryside depopulated as industry drew people away from agriculture. Reformer Ebenezer Howard (1850–1928) believed that the social problems this caused could be prevented by the creation of what he called 'garden cities'. Influenced by Utopian ideals and town-planning practices in America, Howard suggested new towns should be built in the countryside to provide good housing, local employment and plenty of communal amenities. These towns were to be of a limited size and should be surrounded by a permanent green belt.

Model towns had been built before – most famously at Port Sunlight and Bourneville – but these were generally for the workers of one industry and Howard wanted a greater mixture in the population of garden cities. In 1899, Howard set up the Garden City Association and by 1903, First Garden City Ltd had been formed and work on Letchworth had begun, with Barry Parker and Raymond Unwin as architects.

Unwin was to go on to design Hampstead Garden Suburb in 1907, regarded as an ideal planned town but a step away from Howard's principles; he believed a garden city should be an independent settlement rather than the suburb of a larger town or city. Howard did propose the setting up of smaller towns around, but separate from, a larger central community; in 1920 he founded Welwyn Garden City, about 12 miles south of Letchworth.

Hartwell House
Ostensibly a Georgian house but with a surviving Jacobean entrance front. Worked on by James Gibbs, Henry Keene and James Wyatt; restored in the 1980s by Eric Throssell.

Hatfield House
The Jacobean palace of the 1st Earl of Salisbury. Built in the early 17th century to an E-plan, with a Renaissance loggia and classical frontispiece, attributed to Inigo Jones.

Hatfield Old Palace
The remains of a medieval re-brick palace and Tudor royal-family home. All but the hall range was demolished when Salisbury built Hatfield House next door.

Hertford College
First founded in 1740 and then re-founded in 1874. It is most famous for the 'Bridge of Sighs', built in 1914 to link the old quad to newer buildings on the north side of New College Street.

Houghton House
Ruin of a Jacobean mansion, left to decay since the late 18th century. The remnants of Renaissance frontispieces can still be seen, with evidence of a Tuscan-style loggia.

Hughenden Manor
A Georgian house altered and gothicized in the 19th century when it became the home of eminent Victorian politician, Benjamin Disraeli; now preserved as it was in his time.

Jesus College
Founded in 1571, the building of this college did not begin until 1617. Although Jacobean in date, it is Tudor-Gothic in style. Later buildings are in keeping with this style.

Keble College
College founded in 1868 and named after one of the founders of the Oxford Movement. Designed by William Butterfield in High-Victorian, Gothic-Revival style.

Kelmscott Manor
A 16th-century Cotswold manor house with 17th-century additions, leased to the Father of the Arts-and-Crafts movement, William Morris. Maintained today as a shrine to his creative talents.

Kingston Bagpuize House
An early Georgian red-brick house built on the site of an earlier building, it was probably the work of the Townesend family of architects who were based in Oxford.

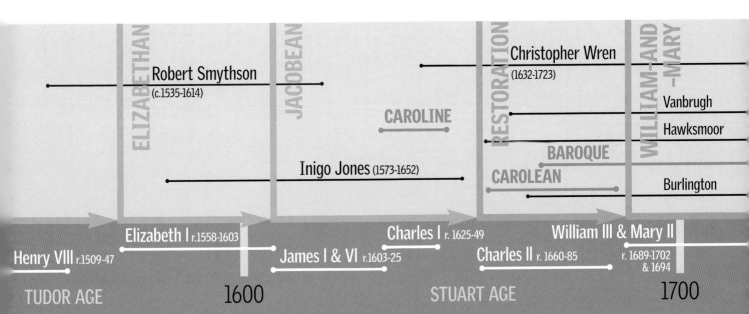

Lancelot 'Capability' Brown (1716-1783)

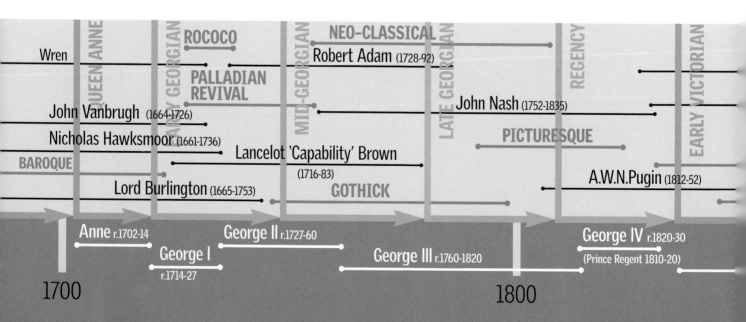

Born in 1716 in Northumberland, Brown began his career as a gardener's boy, moving south in 1740 to work on the gardens at Stowe House (see page 62). By 1749 he was a landscape gardener and, occasionally, an architect. He developed an informal style, creating a gently rolling landscape of wide lawns, punctuated by clumps of trees and his trademark serpentine lakes. He designed over 170 gardens; among his most notable are those at Blenheim Palace (see page 104), Chatsworth House, Longleat, Alnwick Castle and Nuneham Courtenay (see page 140). His landscapes were designed to compliment the houses they surrounded and were the ideal setting for Palladian country villas. As an architect, the buildings Brown designed were Palladian in style; his best surviving houses are Croome Court and Claremont House.

Brown earned his nickname through his habit of assuring clients that their grounds had the 'capability' to be beautifully landscaped. His desire to create gardens that 'improved' nature earned him both praise and criticism; on his death, an obituary claimed 'so closely did he copy nature that his works will be mistaken'.

Knebworth House
Originally a Tudor courtyard house that was altered in the 17th, 18th and 19th centuries; its style today is predominantly Victorian gothic and includes interiors by J.G. Crace.

Letchworth: 296 Norton Way South
Designed by Barry Parker and Raymond Unwin, this was the house where Sir Ebenezer Howard's garden-city principles were first put into practice.

Lincoln College
A medieval college, founded in 1427 by Richard Fleming, Bishop of Lincoln; the contemporary quad survives. The Jacobean chapel is Gothic in style but with Renaissance decoration.

Magdalen College
Founded in 1458, it is a college in two parts; medieval quads and cloisters with a Georgian range on the other side of a deer park. The bell-tower is an Oxford feature.

Mapledurham House
An Elizabethan mansion on the banks of the Thames, built close by the original medieval manor house and church. The interiors reflect several centuries of one family's occupation.

Merton College
Founded in 1274, its Mob Quad includes the some of the oldest residential college buildings in Oxford, dating from 1304. The Jacobean quad has a Renaissance frontispiece.

Milton Manor House
Restoration mansion built after 1663 in the Dutch style. Flanking wings were added in 1764, along with some Gothick interiors.

Minster Lovell Hall
Ruined remains of a great house that dates back to the 1430s, standing on the banks of the River Windrush. Evidence of a Great Hall, solar and Great Chamber survive.

Moor Park
A house begun in the 1720s by Sir James Thornhill and reputedly finished by Giacomo Leoni. The great hall features a trompe l'œil dome and mural of mythological subjects.

Nether Winchenden House
A medieval house, once in monastic ownership, extended by its Tudor owners and give Gothick additions in the 18th century.

New College
Founded in 1379 by the influential William of Wykeham, the college was built on monastic lines with chapel, hall, lodgings and cloisters built around a quadrangle.

Nuffield College
Founded in 1937 by Oxford entrepreneur and philanthropist, Lord Nuffield. Architect Austen Harrison designed a modern building with traditional elements, faced in Cotswold stone.

Nuffield Place
A house built in 1914 that became the home of Lord Nuffield, motoring pioneer and philanthropist. Kept as an example of a comfortable, upper-middle-class, 20th-century home.

Nuneham Courtenay
A Palladian country villa by Stiff Leadbetter set in grounds by Capability Brown that lead down to the River Thames. Brown also worked on parts of the interior.

Old Warden Park
A massive Victorian mansion, built in Jacobethan style and designed by Henry Clutton. Home to a good collection of impressive Victorian paintings.

Old Warden Park: Swiss Cottage
A garden summer house in the style of a Swiss chalet, with thatched roof and rough-hewn wood exterior. The only room still has a fireplace and chimney

Olney: Cowper's House
The home of poet William Cowper, comprised of a row of Jacobean town houses. Now a museum to Cowper and fellow hymn writer, John Newton.

Oriel College
Founded in 1326 by Adam de Brome in honour of Edward II and rebuilt in 1642 in Renaissance style. The library is by James Wyatt.

Pembroke College
College founded in 1624; the Old Quad is Jacobean, the Chapel quad is dominated by the Victorian Gothic-style hall.

The Queen's College
Founded in 1341 and rebuilt at the end of the 17th century. The Front Quad, begun in 1709, was by George Clarke and William Townesend in a French-inspired classical style.

Rousham Park
A Jacobean house remodelled by William Kent in 18th-century Gothic-revival style. The grounds, landscaped by Kent, are the finest example of his work in this field to have survived.

Timeline:

Wren

QUEEN ANNE

EARLY GEORGIAN

ROCOCO

MID-GEORGIAN

NEO-CLASSICAL
Robert Adam (1728-92)

LATE GEORGIAN

REGENCY

EARLY VICTORIAN

PALLADIAN REVIVAL

John Vanbrugh (1664-1726)

Nicholas Hawksmoor (1661-1736)

John Nash (1752-1835)

PICTURESQUE

BAROQUE

Lancelot 'Capability' Brown (1716-83)

A.W.N. Pugin (1812-52)

Lord Burlington (1665-1753)

GOTHICK

Anne r.1702-14

George I r.1714-27

George II r.1727-60

George III r.1760-1820

George IV r.1820-30
(Prince Regent 1810-20)

1700

1800

St Catherine's College
A 1960s college by Danish architect, Arne Jacobsen, in Modernist style. Strictly geometrical in design and minimalist in decoration.

St Edmund Hall
The last academic hall in Oxford, founded in 1278, it became a college in 1957. A small college, based round Front Quad, it has a 17th-century, Oxford-Baroque style old library.

St John's College
Founded in 1555 around an earlier medieval college, parts of which remain. Canterbury Quad, built in 1631, has Renaissance frontispieces.

Shaw's Corner
An Edwardian Arts-and-Crafts style house, built in 1902 and home to George Bernard Shaw from 1906 until his death in 1950; preserved much as the author left it.

Shipton-under-Wychwood: Shaven Crown
A guesthouse attached to a 15th century monastery. It became a hunting lodge after the Dissolution; ranges were added in the 16th and 17th centuries.

Stoke Park
House built in parkland already landscaped by Capability Brown. Begun in 1789 by architect Robert Nasmith; on his death the work was taken over by James Wyatt.

Stonor
An ancient house with 13th-century hall and solar. Extended in the 14th and 16th centuries and georgianized and gothicized in the 18th.

Stowe House
Palatial grandeur and a masterpiece of classical proportion, created by various architects, including Vanbrugh, Kent, Leoni and Adam. Now a school, some magnificent interiors survive.

Stowe Park: Gothic Temple
One of the 25 structures that punctuate Stowe's landscaped grounds. A triangular building of 1741–2, designed in Perpendicular Gothic style by James Gibbs.

Taplow Court
A Jacobean house transformed in the 18th century by Stiff Leadbetter. Re-converted to a Jacobean style by William Burn in the 19th century and extended by one storey.

Chinoiserie

Chinoiserie is the imitation in Western art and architecture of Chinese – or what is perceived to be Chinese – decorative style. It first appeared in Europe in the 17th century and rose to great popularity by the 18th. Falling out of favour towards the end of that century, when tastes became more classical, it enjoyed a revival in the early 1800s.

The earliest manifestation of chinoiserie was in ceramic art; Dutch 17th-century pottery was heavily influenced by imported Chinese blue-and-white porcelain. The use of Chinese-style shapes and decorative motifs became increasingly popular and probably the most famous design in china – willow pattern – is an ideal example of chinoiserie. Created by Thomas Minton in c1790, the pattern was an English interpretation of Chinese style that claimed to illustrate a romantic Chinese legend.

By the 18th century, all the decorative arts reflected an interest in Chinese art. Motifs such as exotic birds, stylized trees and flowers, pagoda-like buildings and fretwork patterns were being incorporated into furniture, fabrics, carpets and interior decor. The profusion of decoration used in chinoiserie style fitted perfectly with the Rococo style so popular in the 18th century. Chinese-inspired motifs were less common in architecture – although the Royal Pavilion Brighton is the notable exception to this rule – and seemed to remain the preserve of garden pavilions, such as the Pagoda in Kew Gardens.

Trinity College
Founded in 1555 on the site of an academic hall, remains of which are seen in Durham Quad. Sir Christopher Wren is thought to have approved the design of the chapel of 1691.

University College
Founded in 1249; built around two quads. Front quad started in 1634, the second begun in 1719 imitating the Tudor Gothic style of the first.

Waddesdon Manor
Late Victorian Rothschild mansion in the style of a French Renaissance chateau. Inside is a famous collection of furniture, furnishings and fine art.

Wadham College
A Jacobean college, founded in 1610, and built in traditional Oxford Tudor-Gothic style around quads. The buildings remained unchanged until the 20th century.

West Wycombe Park
Georgian house owned by Sir Francis Dashwood, inspired by his Grand Tours. The Hell-Fire Club met in caves in the landscaped grounds.

Weston Manor
A 16th-century manor house restored in the 19th century. The Tudor courtyard remains, with the range of a further courtyard still in evidence.

Woburn Abbey
Ancestral seat of the Bedford family, set in a Repton landscape. Parts of the house are 17th-century, with ranges added in the 18th century by Henry Flitcroft and Henry Holland.

Woodhall Park
A Georgian house designed by Thomas Leverton for an absent East-India-Company nabob. Inside is one of the finest examples of a print room to have survived since the 18th century.

Worcester College
Founded in 1714 on the site of an earlier college, the new buildings were by Nicholas Hawksmoor and George Clarke. Part of the college is formed by remaining medieval buildings.

Wrest Park House
A palatial French-style mansion, built in the 1830s and based on the Hôtel de Matignon in Paris. Interiors in the style of Louis XV, the hall is hung with Kneller portraits.

Wrest Park Pavilion
One of Thomas Archer's few surviving buildings. Dating from 1709, it was based on a Borromini church in Rome. The interior is decorated with particularly fine trompe l'œil murals.

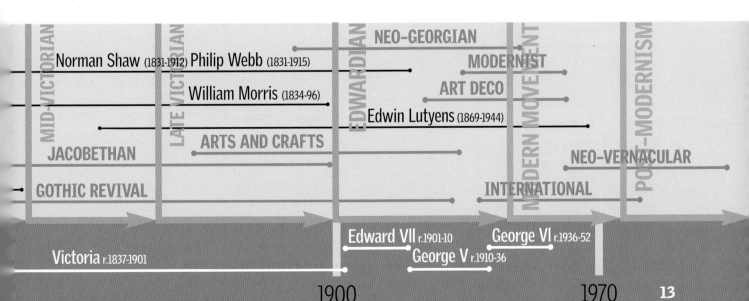

Bedford

Houghton House

Bedfordshire

shire

Bedford: Castle close

✩✩ Victorian villa with re-created interiors

Castle Lane, Bedford; museum, open all year

Where would art be without younger sons? Cecil Higgins, son of the owner of a Bedfordshire brewery, went up to London and spent his inheritance on art. He eventually returned to assume control of the family firm. On his retirement he decided to bequeath his house, Castle Close, as a museum to his native town. He died in 1941.

The house was a classical villa built in the 1840s. Its trustees afforded it scant respect and pulled down some of its internal walls to create an 'open-plan' museum. When in the 1970s they extended the museum into a purpose-built gallery next door, they restored the Higgins house as a Victorian mansion. By then few of the rooms had four surviving walls. An open-plan Victorian mansion is a contradiction in terms but, as a custodian said to me, 'We were stuck with it.' Perhaps some judicious rebuilding might be in order.

That said, Castle Close is a good re-creation of a late-Victorian interior. The intention is 'to give the impression that the family has just gone out for a walk and will be back any minute'. Apart from the lack of walls, this impression is spoilt only by visitors not being allowed to use the stairs, but having to return to the museum and re-enter the top floor through one of the connected galleries.

'The room is a delight,

Left At the heart of the Burges Room is the bed in which the Victorian architect died in 1881. Both the bed and matching dressing table, designed by Burgess c1867, came from his Kensington home. Made of mahogany, they are decorated with paintings and carvings, and inlaid with shell, tinsel and painted glass. **Above** In re-creating a typical Victorian home, the museum has presented the drawing room as the realm of their 'lady of the house'. Here, it is imagined, she would receive visitors and take tea in front of the fire, surrounded by the highly fashionable and heavily decorated furnishings.

The sequence begins downstairs with the oak-panelled smoking room, with wall lights by Norman Shaw and fire irons by Charles Voysey. Beyond are the drawing room and the White Room, the latter with a rosewood cabinet by Gillow and a Tompion clock. The furniture is not uniformly Victorian. There is a Georgian satinwood writing desk and an inlaid Carolean table. But Higgins was primarily a collector of Pre-Raphaelite and Arts and Crafts work. His taste in ceramics decorates every shelf. The library bookcase is by Alfred Waterhouse.

The pride of the upstairs is a bedroom, created as a tribute to the neo-Gothic architect, William Burges. The room is dark yet colourful, and includes a superb bookcase, dressing table and bed, all designed by Burges. Panels on the wardrobe, again by Burges, illustrate the clothing of Adam; below are paintings of anthropomorphic toiletries, with dancers in the form of toothbrushes and combs. The room is a delight, executed with levity and humour.

This is more than can be said for the guide-book which is saturated with political correctness. We must apparently be told that the late Victorians persecuted women and servants. A man's word was 'law'. Women were not allowed to smoke, were forced to 'love, honour and obey' and talked only of social tittle-tattle. It makes us wonder how Queen Victoria, Florence Nightingale and Sarah Bernhardt survived their long, tedious and oppressed existences.

executed with **levity and humour.'**

Left Among the surviving features at Bushmead Priory is the stained glass of the southeast window. The refectory and parts of the kitchen and cloister remain today; the priory's church, infirmary and chapter house have long since disappeared. After the Dissolution, Bushmead was converted to secular use and then passed first to Sir William Gascoigne, Cardinal Wolsey's Controller of the Household, and then to William Gery.

Bushmead priory

⭐ Remains of an Augustinian priory in a Bedfordshire valley

6 miles NE of Bedford; English Heritage, open part year by arrangement

Bushmead is included here for its setting as much as its content. The old Augustinian priory sat in a secluded valley deep in the Bedfordshire farmland. What is left sits there still, accompanied by a Georgian farmhouse next door and a half-timbered one across the valley. Bushmead is supremely peaceful in a county sadly short of that quality.

The building accessible today is the old priory refectory. It has a Gothic doorway and Tudor windows, apparently with their original wooden tracery. The roof is intact and covers a tall, single-storeyed hall with cobbled floor. This has a two-storey section beyond, presumably the prior's private rooms. This must have been a cosy, gentle retreat.

On the first floor are wall-paintings and some stained glass. They suggest that, as in other cases elsewhere after the Dissolution, new owners showed the old buildings and their decoration a measure of respect. At last, we do so too.

Houghton house

⭐ Ruin of a Jacobean mansion with Renaissance frontispieces

Near Ampthill, 8 miles S of Bedford; English Heritage, open all year

Houghton is a most romantic ruin. The Middle Ages built houses in dells and by streams, with an eye to seclusion and security. The Elizabethans and Jacobeans were prepared to flaunt their wealth; if they could find a hill they would build on it. Houghton House was commissioned in 1615 by Mary, Countess of Pembroke, sister of Sir Philip Sidney, and an accomplished patron of the arts and horses. It looks out north over Bedfordshire. The scenery is now poxed with brickwork chimneys. The house, roofless but with its walls standing, lies at the end of a long, almost overgrown beech avenue. Although the brickworks have eroded its fabric, it retains its pride. It was reputedly the basis for Bunyan's 'House Beautiful' in *Pilgrim's Progress*.

The house was bought in 1738 by the Duke of Bedford for his son, the Marquis of Tavistock, but it was stripped and sold in 1794, some years after the Marquis's death. The destruction was conducted, according to one account, 'with the delight of a butcher killing sheep'. The place has been a ruin ever since, but the building remains stylistically intriguing. Houghton House is a conventional Jacobean H-plan mansion with prominent corner towers, bay windows and large gables. Yet three of the façades have, or mostly had, sophisticated Renaissance frontispieces of the sort still relatively unusual outside the court circle of Inigo Jones.

These frontispieces are barely discernible, although they are clear in the print of the old house on display on the site. One elevation retains a Tuscan loggia, with some of its metopes surviving. Other bits and pieces can be detected, a keystone here, a medallion there, all teasing ghosts of what was clearly a remarkable composition. The Victorians would have taken this building in hand and given it back its historical form. We dare do no more than stabilize it.

Old Warden park

6 miles SE of Bedford; private house, exterior accessible part year, interior open by arrangement

Joseph Shuttleworth was a Victorian businessman from Lincolnshire eager to move up in the world. In 1872 he bought the Old Warden estate of some 4,600 acres from the family of Lord Ongley. Shuttleworth pulled down the old house and hired the London architect, Henry Clutton, to design a new one. The design he cheekily if vaguely modelled on Gawthorpe, the Lancashire house of Lord Shuttleworth, to whom he was no relation. The reaction of the Lancashire Shuttleworths is not recorded. Old Warden is far bigger than Gawthorpe, the Jacobethan style at its most grandiloquent. The house is truly a Victorian pile.

In 1940, Joseph Shuttleworth's daughter-in-law, Dorothy, decided to commemorate the death of her son in a flying accident with a trust devoted to his two interests, aviation and agriculture. The Shuttleworth Trust is now an agricultural college, while its hangars hold Britain's finest collection of antique airplanes. Dorothy Shuttleworth continued to live in the house and preside over the college, welcoming each new student personally until her death in 1968. The planes take part in regular flying displays overhead. On my last visit an 'aerial prom' was rehearsing, a falconry school was in progress and a wedding was taking place inside.

The house entrance is directly into a large hall, off which lead an even grander staircase hall and formal saloon, now a banqueting hall. The ceilings are all neo-Jacobean and the fireplaces gigantic, tiled and with reliefs of hunting scenes.

Old Warden is most remarkable for its pictures, collected by the Shuttleworths with no great imagination but a fine sense of scale. It is a gallery of grandiloquent country house art. Apart from a Lawrence, the artists are Victorians only now emerging from obscurity, such as William Leader, Vicat Cole, Edwin Long and Frank Dicksee. Their works, mostly romantic landscapes, society portraits and 'stags at bay', are on a hundred country house walls.

Swiss cottage

★ Romantic chalet at the heart of an enchanted garden

At Old Warden Park, 6 miles SE of Bedford; private house and garden, open all year

When I first glimpsed the chalet at Old Warden Park, it was a warm summer day. A party was making its nervous way through the woods and out into a glade; above it stood a cottage on a knoll. It was a surreal scene worthy of Tolkien.

The chalet lies at the centre of the Swiss Garden, distinguishable from an English one only by a scatter of Swiss-style buildings erected in the 1820s. Nearby is a romantic grotto, ornamental bridge and thatched canopy over a seat running round the trunk of an oak tree. The seat was reputedly where a beautiful Swiss girl caught a cold in a rainstorm and later died.

The garden was designed by Lord Ongley, then owner of Old Warden Park (see opposite), and reflects the *cottage orné* style of many of the new houses built by Ongley in the neighbouring village. The architect is believed to be J. B. Papworth of St Neot's, publisher of *Hints on Ornamental Gardening* and a promoter of the style.

The Swiss Cottage is no more than a single-room summer house, but of peculiar charm. It has a thatched conical roof and distinctive porch. A balcony runs round the outside, resting on untreated upright logs. The outside is panelled in hazel twigs and the inside is covered in fretwork. The craftsmanship is excellent. The interior has a fireplace and chimney. A fierce peacock guards the door.

Woburn abbey

★ ★ ★ ★ Principal home of the Bedfords since the early 17th century

At Woburn, 6 miles SE of Milton Keynes; private house, open part year

Woburn is Bedfordshire's one great house and makes the most of it. In the 1950s, the then Duke of Bedford pioneered the movement to save such mansions, in his case by opening the house fully to the public and creating a safari park and other attractions in the grounds. A true showman, he would dance the twist with the local dairy maids and lunch in the Canaletto Room while visitors walked past behind ropes. Today's Woburn is more restrained, though the personality of the family remains dominant, which is as it should be. The guidebook makes full use of the first person singular.

Nothing could be more serene than the approach. From the village of Woburn, the drive leads through an evergreen wood thick with cedar, fir, pine and yew. Suddenly it bursts out onto a Repton landscape of spacious parkland, across which deer drift like clouds. Visitors then drive round the outskirts of the U-shaped house, admiring the west front built by Henry Flitcroft in 1746–61 and south front added by Henry Holland forty years later. The north range remains mostly 17th century. Despite this variety, the house seems of a piece, stately but unostentatious.

To the rear of the Abbey are two large quadrangular courts also built by Flitcroft. They were once linked by a building containing tennis courts, a riding school, stables and ancillary offices. Since the present U-shaped main house once had a fourth side, Woburn was a very large property indeed. In 1950, decay was used to justify demolishing Flitcroft's

'... a Repton landscape of **spacious parkland**

riding school and Holland's east range, destruction unthinkable today. Yet Flitcroft's surviving quadrangles are still among the finest outbuildings of any great house.

The route through the house is not wholly satisfactory. Visitors enter from behind into the old 17th-century rooms. This means first encountering not a Great Hall but an ante-room of the sort in which a tenant might meet the Duke's agent. That said, the Book Room contains a superb collection of natural history books, some helpfully open to view. Here too is a copy of the Althorp van Dyck, of the youthful brothers-in-law, the Duke of Bedford and Earl of Bristol, who were to take opposing sides in the Civil War.

A corridor called Paternoster Row leads to Flitcroft's staircase. The walls are lined with family portraits, dominated on the stairs by a van Dyck of the 5th Countess of Bedford with a tiny dog. The rooms now become more spacious, although at Woburn never losing touch with domesticity. They are pleasantly filled with family memorabilia.

Along the Dukes' Corridor is a room dedicated to the Flying Duchess, wife of the 11th Duke. A traveller, naturalist and photographer, she was a celebrated aviator between the wars, flying both to India and to the Cape but was killed in 1937 crashing in the Fens. The Yellow Drawing Room has a spectacular Rococo ceiling and overmantel. It was decorated for the 4th Duke in the 1760s in the French style, to commemorate his ambassadorship to Paris. The so-called Racing Room was decorated by Flitcroft in the same style, and is now a shrine to the present family's enthusiasm for horse racing. The purple and white Bedford racing colours are draped over 18th-century furniture in what seems a studied anachronism. Instead of Bedford humans we now see Bedford horses and their jockeys.

across which deer drift like clouds.'

Left In 1747 the 4th Duke commissioned Henry Flitcroft to create Woburn's state apartments. The main bedroom of the suite became known as Queen Victoria's Bedroom after her 1841 visit. Woburn has had a history of royal visits; Elizabeth I stayed during the time of the 2nd Earl (1527–85) and Charles I and his queen visited in 1636. **Below** Woburn's grotto takes the form of a north-facing loggia and was built between 1619 and 1641 for the 4th Earl and his family as a retreat where they could enjoy the fresh air but escape the heat of the day. In the mid-17th century, however, the grotto was felt to be too cold and the openings were filled in with glazed panels; today, these are plate-glass windows.

Flitcroft's state rooms along the west front move up a scale in grandeur. They begin with the bedroom in which Queen Victoria stayed in 1841. The ceiling is higher, the decoration more ornate. The Queen's Dressing Room has blue walls and paintings by Jan Steen, Cuyp and van Dyck. The Blue Drawing Room claims to be where 'afternoon tea' was first celebrated in the early 19th century. A table is laid for this delicate refreshment, overlooked by Claude and Canaletto.

The state saloon, the chief reception room, rises two storeys in the centre of the west range. Its silk wall-hangings were so faded when the house was first opened to the public that they had to be removed. Rather than replace them in kind, the then Duke commissioned Roland Pym to paint scenes from Russell history as murals. They will take time to merge into the context. Beyond is the state dining room, lined with van Dycks, and at the end of the enfilade, the celebrated Canaletto room. Redecorated and with its Venetian window restored, the walls shimmer with Venetian light and colour.

The south wing by Henry Holland is privately occupied. Visitors must return down Flitcroft's Long Gallery, divided by Corinthian columns as if into three rooms. It contains a display of 16th- and 17th-century portraits. These include the Earl of Essex by Gheeraerts and the famous Armada portrait of Elizabeth I. Her hand sits proprietorially on a globe, while the Spanish fleet lies wrecked on the rocks behind her. Further Bedford treasures are now housed and displayed in secure basement vaults. They include sets of Meissen, Chelsea and Sèvres, as well as much gold and silver.

The exit is back through the 17th-century wing, including a parlour and grotto. The latter is a superb example of this genre, the gods of classical Rome turned troglodyte. The work is even attributed to Inigo Jones's protégé, Isaac de Caux, who worked for the Bedfords on their Covent Garden estate. The grotto is furnished with chairs in the form of dolphins and shells.

Wrest Park house

★★ Early 19th-century grand mansion, built in a French style

Near Silsoe, 10 miles S of Bedford; English Heritage, open part year

Terrible things were done to Wrest Park by the rerouting of the A6 round the adjacent village of Silsoe. It saved the village but spoilt the park. It reminds me of the old-fashioned obstetrician's question: 'Sir, would you like me to save the mother or the child?' At least drivers can get a glimpse of the house from behind their steering wheels.

Wrest is stylistically remarkable, indeed for its date unique in England. It was built by the Earl de Grey in the 1830s to replace what was the family's ancestral home; de Greys had lived at Wrest since the 13th century. Unlike most English houses over the previous century, it took its cue not from Italy but from France, the earliest such example in the country. The Earl was an ardent francophile. The drive from Silsoe is through grand gateposts and into Normandy.

The house lies on the right of the drive with geometric precision, simple, ashlar-faced and 13 bays long. It has deep windows, mansard roofs and corner pavilions. The model was the Hôtel de Matignon in Paris. The Earl was his own architect but used the French-sounding James Cléphane as his clerk of works. Allocating responsibility between them is impossible. The Earl interfered all the time, claiming that there was not a ladder or a scaffold that he had not climbed to supervise the work.

Above right The central staircase hall at Wrest Park rises up through the full height of the house. The twin flights of the elegant cantilevered staircase climb to a screen of columns on the first floor. A collection of 18th-century portraits are incorporated into the architectural decoration at this level. They include paintings by Godfrey Kneller, Jacopo Amigoni and John Clostermans of members of both the royal and de Grey families.

The style of the interior is Louis XV. The central staircase hall is spectacular, richly ornamented with plaster trophies and relief panels above the doors. It is said that the Earl regarded the plasterwork females as insufficiently well endowed and 'enhanced' them with his own hands. The royal portraits, some by Kneller, are ideal to the setting. The other reception rooms face the garden beyond and form a stately enfilade. They have painted ceilings, with gold and white predominating, and fine fireplaces.

Outside, the Earl's French parterres lie immediately below the garden front. They have been restored as sweeping scrolls of gravel interspersed with flower beds and classical statuary. Ahead stretches the Long Water, Georgian landscaping before the era of Capability Brown, although Brown was employed at Wrest in 1758 to make the canals curve more 'naturally'.

The grounds contain an orangery, banqueting house, Petit Trianon, temples and bridges – a rural version of West London's Chiswick House. At the climax of the Long Water is Thomas Archer's earlier Pavilion (see page 28).

Wrest Park pavilion

★ English Baroque pavilion, designed by Thomas Archer

Near Silsoe, 10 miles S of Bedford; English Heritage, open part year

Left and **above right** The interior of the pavilion at Wrest Park was decorated with astonishing *trompe-l'œil* murals by Louis Hauderoy soon after building work was completed. The paintings complement Archer's architecture. So significant was this building that Colen Campbell included it in his great catalogue of British architecture, the *Vitruvius Britannicus* of 1715. Its importance today lies in its rarity; Archer completed relatively few commissions and the pavilion at Wrest Park is one of only a handful of secular buildings that still remain.

Thomas Archer's Pavilion, designed in 1709 for Earl de Grey's predecessor, the Duke of Kent, is a virtuoso essay in English Baroque. As de Grey was later to take the Parisian *hôtel* as his model for his new Wrest Park (see page 26), in whose grounds the pavilion lies, so Archer took Borromini's St Ivo's church behind Rome's Piazza Navona. It does not soar, as does Borromini.

The Pavilion, restored by English Heritage, is closer to Wren in its English solidity. But it is a minor masterpiece, beautifully set at the end of the canal from de Grey's French château, guarded by a statue of William III in Roman dress.

The building has a large classical portal enclosing a no less grand doorway beneath a giant dome. Matching doorways guard each of the four sides. The circular interior is a superb composition, rising to a cupola. It was painted with architectural *trompe-l'œil* by Louis Hauderoy in 1712. These murals have recently been restored.

The Pavilion was more than a summer-house. It has a series of small bedrooms, one of which has a fireplace. There are kitchens in the basement and a servant's room in the dome, reached by a concealed stair. The house was clearly intended for more than taking tea and might have been used overnight for hunting parties. There is even a two-seater privy.

hamshire

West Wycombe Park

Buckinghamshire

Ascott house

★★★ Victorian Tudorbethan house, crammed with paintings and porcelain

8 miles W of Dunstable; National Trust, open part year

The Rothschilds were to Buckinghamshire what the Cavendishes were to Derbyshire. Their Victorian houses at Waddesdon, Mentmore, Halton and Ascott are grouped together in the Vale of Aylesbury, as if clan proximity were as important at weekends as it was during the week in the City.

Ascott House was a small Tudor farmhouse when it was bought in 1873 as a hunting lodge by Mayer de Rothschild of neighbouring Mentmore. It was converted for Leopold de Rothschild by George Devey and extended in the 1930s for the collector, Anthony de Rothschild, who left it to the National Trust. It is now occupied by Sir Evelyn de Rothschild, and presents the antithesis of ostentatious Waddesdon.

Ascott is an overgrown cottage. It proves the appeal of Tudor to every era and condition of England. The house is a row of half-timbered, heavily gabled bays, supplemented when extra rooms were needed. Nothing is grand, except the splendour of the grounds. Yew hedges, terraces and woods slope languidly towards the distant Chilterns. On one terrace is a box and yew garden, its topiary circle spelling out 'light and shade by turn but love always'.

A fragment of the original house survives in a beam over the front door, dated 1606. Inside is a lateral corridor with the entrance hall beyond. Apart from the grand Common Room, the reception rooms are those of any comfortable country residence.

Not so the paintings. In the hall are Stubbs's *Five Mares* and pictures by Romney and Reynolds. The dining room walls, painted to imitate tiles, display Dutch Old Masters, including Cuyp's *View of Dordrecht*. In the corridor are two delightful paintings of the Rothschilds leaving Frankfurt. One

Below Among the collection of fine art found at Ascott House are several paintings by eminent Dutch artists. The dining room, its walls painted with *trompe l'œil* Dutch tiles, is the perfect setting for masterpieces by Aelbert Cuyp, Adrian van Ostade and Jan Steen.

Left A painting by George Stubbs, *Five Mares*, hangs in the hall at Ascott. Stubbs, a self-taught artist, rose to prominence as a painter of exquisite equine portraits in the 1760s after a series of finely observed anatomical drawings of horses brought him to the attention of several important aristocratic patrons.

shows the Elector entrusting his estate to Mayer, the other the sons taking their leave for Vienna, Naples, Paris and London. The Common Room has a frieze of Victorian maxims such as 'Waste Not Want Not', and Turner's *Cicero's Villa*. The library has a superb Gainsborough, of the red-haired Duchess of Richmond in bright turquoise against a stormy background.

The pride of Ascott is the Chinese porcelain collected by Anthony de Rothschild. I have never seen such work better displayed. It is of all periods, chiefly of the Han, T'ang and Ming dynasties. One room has the porcelain arranged by style and colour, interspersed with Chippendale chairs. From every corner, dragons and demons dart from shelves or niches. They too seem strangely comfortable in these homely surroundings.

Bletchley park

★ Late Victorian mansion and home of World-War-II code busters

At Bletchley, 2 miles S of Milton Keynes; museum, open all year

The role of Bletchley in the Second World War is now acknowledged, but wresting it from the Ministry of Defence took as much effort as wresting Enigma from the Germans. The conversion of the house and outbuildings into a museum of wartime intelligence is not yet complete. For the time being, the place is a monument to military squalor. The epitome of British electronic genius sits in a wilderness of old huts, abandoned jeeps, concrete standings, tarmac, plastic and neon. If you are an old soldier and want all this brought back to life, Bletchley is for you.

The house was that of an eccentric millionaire named Sir Herbert Leon. He bought the estate in 1883 and built a fantasy mansion in eclectic taste. The exterior might be that of a seaside villa in Broadstairs, asymmetrical with Dutch and Tudor gables, a moorish roof and Tudor Gothic embellishments. The inside is similar. The ceilings are almost all reproduction Jacobean. The hall has marble arches and a sumptuous fireplace. The ballroom is astonishing. Linenfold panelling rises to a ceiling of deeply undercut plasterwork on a gilded background, as if pleading for a visit from Elizabeth I.

The house was sold after Lady Leon's death in 1937 and a year later became the base for MI6's communications operation under Sir Richard Gambier-Parry. Throughout the war it was the venue for military intercepts and codebreaking, its best-known coup being the cracking of the German Enigma codes. The work done at Bletchley by the mathematician, Alan Turing, formed the basis of electronic computing. All this is now recorded in the various displays.

Elsewhere on the site visitors can see military vehicles, a 1940s mess, wartime movies and a 'cryptology trail'. Everything is labelled Top Secret and Station X. The guides assert that 'this is where it really happened' so often as to lessen our wonder at what really did happen. The huts also encompass the Milton Keynes Model Railway Society and the Leighton Buzzard Boat Club. It is, in truth, a museum of general clutter.

Boarstall tower

⭐ Medieval gatehouse in garden surrounded by a moat

At Boarstall, 10 miles NE of Oxford; National Trust, open part year

The story begins in the 11th century. A ferocious boar in the king's forest of Bernewood was trapped and killed by a wily forester named Nigel. The grateful Edward the Confessor gave Nigel a horn – now in the archives at Aylesbury – and land on which to build a house. Nigel's family held the house across the entire sweep of English history, until giving it to the National Trust in 1943. Even then the Aubrey-Fletchers rented it back and sublet it to the present custodians.

The old house spread round a central courtyard; this is now a garden surrounded by a moat. All that survives is a noble gatehouse in the form of a tower. This was 'improved' for use as a banqueting house at the end of the 16th century, and includes an upper chamber with windows on all four sides. In a print of 1695, the tower is seen to dominate the old house behind, set in what was then a formal parterre. The property passed through a succession of daughters to the Aubreys, but when a six-year-old Aubrey died of food poisoning in 1777, the grief-stricken family demolished the main house. The tower was left empty and the gardens overgrown for 150 years. Not until 1925 did an Aubrey tenant, Mrs Jennings Bramley, modernize the property and alter the old entrance to make the present dining room.

The tower is reached by a bridge over its remaining moat. The hard lines of 14th-century military architecture are softened by later parapets and oriel windows, notably over the doorway. The garden behind bears traces of a reported visit by Capability Brown. The interior has been spoilt with National Trust heating and health-and-safety regulations, but the thick walls, cosy bedrooms and glimpsed views over the surrounding landscape more than compensate.

The banqueting room above is excellently preserved, with wide windows and a large fireplace. Windows carry heraldic glass and the roof offers a view of the Chiltern escarpment.

John Milton
1608–1674

John Milton was one of the most scholarly of English poets. Master of many languages and student of several disciplines, including theology, philosophy, history and science, he put his learning to good use in both his poetic and political writings. A radical republican, Milton espoused many controversial theories and beliefs and expressed his opinions in several polemical tracts. His poetry also reflected these ideals; in *Paradise Lost*, the epic blank-verse tale of Adam and Eve's fall from grace, Milton conveyed his disappointment in the failure of Cromwell's Commonwealth.

The village is immaculate. Every brick is re-pointed and every hedge clipped. If you stand still too long in Chalfont St Giles, someone will paint you white. When John Milton arrived to escape the Great Plague in 1665, he had been Latin secretary to Cromwell and chief propagandist for the Commonwealth. On the Restoration, aged fifty-seven and already blind, he was evicted from his Westminster home and moved to Bunhill Fields in the City. Now the threat of disease drove him to the Puritan Chilterns. The Quakers were up the road at Jordans. The lord of Chalfont manor was Colonel George Fleetwood, one of the regicides. Milton's reader and pupil, Thomas Ellwood, lived nearby.

Ellwood found the poet a 'pretty box', the tiniest of cottages. Milton's daughters had long exasperated him, and he had married a third time. Old friends and supporters were in prison or abroad. *Paradise Lost* was unfinished. Milton stayed at Chalfont only a year and returned to London when the plague had passed. Yet it was here that he found the peace to complete his epic, and begin *Paradise Regained*. Chalfont is full of Miltonic spirit.

The surviving cottage is a work of simple village architecture. It clings to the roadside opposite the Milton's

Chalfont St Giles: Milton's cottage

★ ★ Poet's Chiltern refuge from London and the Plague

Deanway, Chalfont St Giles; museum, open part year

Head pub and an Indian restaurant, and has retained its garden and adjacent meadow. The garden has a well, water butt, hand bell and 'necessarium' (latrine). The walls are of exposed timbers. Given the commercial potential of the place, the Milton Cottage Trust has kept the building in exemplary condition.

To the right of the present doorway from the garden is Milton's own study. Here Milton not only wrote but also slept, since his blindness prevented him from risking the steps to the upper floor. Here too was his small hand organ. The parlour contains a fine tall-backed chair known to have been owned by Milton, as was the writing table in the study.

The house is kept as a museum. Walls have pictures of Milton and his family, including a Kneller painted from memory shortly after the poet's death. There are first editions of most of Milton's works and, in the parlour, a case displaying them translated into foreign tongues. Despite the passing traffic, birdsong can still be heard through the window. As Wordsworth recalled of Milton at this time, 'Thy soul was like a star and dwelt apart,/ Thou hadst a voice whose sound was like the sea.'

Left Milton's study at Chalfont St Giles became both his bedroom and workplace. The poet had been totally blind for more than ten years by the time he came to the cottage, but his blindness, probably caused by glaucoma, did not impede his work; he continued to write, aided by several amanuenses, including the poet Andrew Marvell. Milton's greatest works, *Paradise Lost*, *Paradise Regained* and *Samuel Agonistes*, were all written long after he had lost his sight.

Chenies manor

✦ ✧ Ancestral Tudor home of the Bedford family

At Chenies, 6 miles W of Watford; private house, open part year

The Russells, Dukes of Bedford, are still buried in the church at Chenies. The family may have moved, to London, Woburn and elsewhere, but in death they return here. You can take a man from his roots, but not the roots from a man.

The manor came into the Russell family by virtue of the marriage in 1526 of John Russell to the then heiress of Chenies. John Russell came from Dorset and was a rising star at court, favoured servant of both Henry VII and VIII, later created Earl of Bedford and awarded Woburn Abbey (see page 22) by Edward VI. He rebuilt the medieval hall house at Chenies with diapered brickwork and decorative chimneys. The house was used by the Russells into the 17th century, and was later occupied by their steward. It was then modernized by Edward Blore in 1829 for a younger Russell but since 1957 has been in the hands of the MacLeod Matthews family, who look after it well. The formal garden specializes in tulips, which splendidly fill every room in season.

Above Queen Elizabeth I knew Chenies Manor well and had first visited in 1534 with her parents, Henry VIII and Anne Boleyn, when just a baby. The parlour in which she is believed to have worked when staying at the house is now known as Queen Elizabeth's room. In the grounds stands an ancient oak, reputedly the Queen's favourite spot at Chenies and the place where, legend has it, she once lost some jewellery.

The house is L-shaped round the front courtyard. The present entrance lies directly ahead with an octagonal staircase tower and prominent stepped gables. The original hall has been buried in later alterations, with only its solar cross-wing surviving. John Russell appears to have commenced alterations in the late 1520s. The principal downstairs room is now the Tudor parlour, with a wide fireplace arch and beamed ceiling. The coat of arms over the fire is carved of wood blown down in the gale of 1987.

Next door is an old chaplain's room, with beyond it a series of Blore interiors containing Georgian and later furniture. These are very much family living rooms. The upstairs bedrooms are effusively furnished in bright colours and four-posters. Queen Elizabeth's Room is said to be the chamber in which she worked when visiting Chenies on tour. It has a fine tapestry chair. The Pink Bedroom has a small oratory with tiny priest's hole, a charming survival.

The side wing of Chenies was the guest wing of the old Tudor house. The billiard room was once probably the Great Chamber. It is hung in William Morris wallpaper and family portraits. The attic is the most atmospheric space in the house. It was once the armoury and sleeping quarters for soldiers and servants and runs the length of the wing, full of ghosts.

Chiltern Open Air museum

2 miles W of Rickmansworth; museum, open part year

Chiltern is a museum dedicated, like the Avoncroft and Weald and Downland museums, to rescuing vernacular architecture and recreating it in something like its original rural setting. This work merits all support, since such buildings are the most vulnerable of all relics of English architecture.

Amersham prefab ★★

originally at Finch Lane Estate, Amersham

Working-class houses vanish faster than any other. They are the least valuable and most readily victims to the bulldozer. A few have been rescued and rebuilt, precious memorials to the early post-war way of life. We have a hundred Georgian mansions but precious few prefabs.

The term is short for 'prefabricated temporary bungalow'. Half a million were planned immediately after the Second World War, being built largely from aircraft factories no longer in use. Fewer than 160,000 were built, in part because (as with all government projects) they cost more than conventional homes supplied by the private sector. Priced at £1,300 and rented for 13 shillings a

Left The prefab at the Chiltern Open Air Museum was one of 46 such structures that were made in Rickmansworth and then erected at Finch Lane in Amersham shortly after the end of World War II. Although intended only as a temporary home, the bungalow remained occupied until 1987 when it was replaced by new housing. Today, the preserved prefab is furnished much as it would have been in the late 1940s, with utility furniture, textured upholstery and fittings – such as the fireplace – from that era.

week, they compared badly even with local council houses at £450 or 5 shillings a week. Some survive in parts of South London.

The 'Universal House, Mark 3' may seem little better than a caravan without wheels to the modern eye, yet the houses were up-to-date in comparison with tenements or Victorian back-to-backs. The building consisted of two bedrooms, a living room and a kitchen, with a small bathroom and separate toilet. It was connected to electricity. Here everything is in place, except that one bedroom has sadly been replaced with an exhibition.

The house has been decorated in its original cream and green and fitted with authentic kit. The bedroom is dishevelled, apparently to appeal to children. The sitting room comes with flying ducks, sewing machine, coal stove and utility furniture. In the kitchen is a Belling cooker, washing copper, mangle and Electrolux fridge. The garden retains its rabbit hutch and tool-shed. I can already imagine the place as a fashion icon.

AIR MUSEUM

High Wycombe Toll house ✳

originally at Oxford Road, High Wycombe

These houses once dotted the roadsides of England. The toll house is the exact precursor of the motorway tollbooth, and collected money from stage coaches and other road users on behalf of the 18th-century turnpike trusts which were charged with maintaining their local high roads. Toll keepers were as unpopular as traffic wardens. They were seen as tax collectors and were regularly robbed. Their houses were therefore designed as mini-fortresses. This one has iron bars and shutters on all its windows and even crenellation round its roof. The house was given to the museum in 1977 after being hit by a passing (or not-passing) lorry.

The building has been re-erected with road, gate, fence and garden. Inside is an office-cum-living room, set out to receive tolls. Behind is the bedroom with iron bedstead and patchwork quilt. Kitchen, wash house and privy are to the rear. A family of five lived here in 1841. It would not have looked so twee then. On busy days, a toll-keeper in full costume – not a waxwork – is on hand to direct visitors and lend the place authenticity.

Leagrave cottages ✳

originally at Compton Avenue, Leagrave

These two cottages, in effect one house, were situated by a busy road in Leagrave. The building was an early 18th-century thatched barn. This was converted into two cottages later that century by inserting partitions and a brick chimneystack. Declared unfit for human habitation in 1982, it has been reconstructed as in the 1920s. The downstairs living and eating rooms are extremely simple. A small range has a kettle, an iron and a few pots. Oil lamps hang on the walls, the floor is of scrubbed brick.

The only signs of comfort are a battered leather armchair, a pipe rack and a Bible. A row of war medals and a couple of cheap prints decorate the wall. The room looks wholly original. The privy is in the garden. The lean-to was a kitchen but Leagrave locals said it was previously a cobbler's workshop and so it has been restored as such. The garden has been planted with simple cottage flowers, some herbs and rhubarb.

Chilton house

★★ Georgian mansion built in Queen-Anne style

At Chilton, 9 miles W of Aylesbury; private house, open by arrangement

Chilton's façade, looking out across the fields of the Vale of Aylesbury, is supremely comforting. It is a 1740s remodelling of an earlier manor of the Croke family, itself rebuilt in 1705. The present façade is distinctly 'Queen Anne' in style. Brick walls have long pilasters and prominent windows with Gibbs surrounds, their keystones like popping eyebrows. Steps lead down to a lawned courtyard with flanking pavilions and a sumptuous wrought-iron gate.

The builder was a judge, Richard Carter, who wanted no truck with the new Whig Palladians. In those days, architecture was also politics. To the judge, certainty lay with redbrick and rustication. Architectural purists would consider them anachronisms.

The house passed to the Aubrey family (see Boarstall Tower, page 35) but decayed in the 19th and 20th centuries and was lucky to survive at all. It was a school during the Second World War and then a council nursing home. The current generation of Aubrey-Fletchers run it as a 'country house' convalescent home, mercifully saving a house destined for demolition.

Unlike the exterior, the interior is that of a conventional mansion of the mid-18th century. The entrance hall is decorated in soft yellows and whites. Fluted pilasters and broken pediments adorn the walls and the ceiling plasterwork is intact. The grand staircase survives beyond and the main sitting room has Rococo plasterwork. Behind lies the church and estate village.

Claydon house

★★★★ Remaining wing of a magnificent Georgian mansion with extraordinary interiors

At Middle Claydon, 14 miles NW of Aylesbury; National Trust, open part year

Claydon contains the most stunning interiors in England. It is a riposte to all who may find mid-Georgian houses dull. The house was built by Ralph, Earl Verney, to outshine his political rival, Earl Temple, at neighbouring Stowe. The contest was to bankrupt them. They both eventually had to live abroad to escape their creditors.

In 1757 Verney commissioned as architect a carver named Luke Lightfoot, a decision he was to regret. After ten years of work, relations between them collapsed, in part on a matter of money and in part on a matter of style. The building was hugely expensive, while Verney's contemporaries did not admire Lightfoot's extravagant Rococo.

The gentleman-Palladian, Sir Thomas Robinson, was appalled at 'such a work as the world never saw', and pleaded with Verney to change course in favour of Adam's stuccoist, Joseph Rose. Eventually Verney lost his nerve and sacked Lightfoot, suing him for uncompleted decorations. The carver settled in Dulwich, and his son emigrated to Australia where Lightfoots remain to this day. I am told that they still call a son 'Verney' in each generation.

Robinson was now asked by Verney to pick up the pieces, but it was too late. Verney's flight to escape his creditors was tragic. Shortly before his death in 1791, he was found wandering through the shuttered, cobwebbed rooms of Claydon, doubtless

Left An octagonal table depicting the god Bacchus in the library at Claydon was made by G. Ciuli, c1825. It was made using the terrazzo technique, whereby an image was created from small chips of different coloured marble. The table was bought in Italy by Sir Harry Verney, 2nd Baronet (1801–94). Sir Harry, originally a Calvert, assumed the name Verney on inheriting Claydon House in 1827. The library was redecorated by his second wife Parthenope, who was the sister of Florence Nightingale.

musing on the terrors that architects hold in store for those who put their faith in them. Verney's niece demolished two-thirds of the completed mansion, the present house being a remaining wing. But later Verneys cared for the place and passed it to the National Trust in 1956.

The original house was three times the size of the present building and must indeed have rivalled Stowe. The exterior of the present wing is modest. An elegant seven-bay west front looks out over a landscaped park with an arched central section. There are just two storeys, stone faced with side elevations of brick.

The explosion occurs inside. The North Hall was locked when I first visited Claydon but I was able to peer in. It was like Sleeping Beauty beneath a dust-sheet, light filtering through cracks in the shutters. Lightfoot worked initially with Verney's close collaboration. His sources were German Rococo pattern books, borrowing freely from Gothick and chinoiserie.

The hall is encrusted with broken pediments over doors. Mirrors and mantelpieces are festooned with swags, drapes, Ho-Ho birds, fronds and cornucopias. The Rococo shell is everywhere, defying symmetry with poise, light and joyfulness. The room transcends style, a decorative programme born of a desire solely to delight the eye. The carvings were done in Lightfoot's Southwark studio but painted *in situ*. It is said that he never saw the room complete.

The next room is the saloon, also by Lightfoot and only a little more restrained. The six doors are classical and the fireplace is surrounded by tumbling putti, supposedly illustrating the invention of the Corinthian order from an acanthus leaf. The ceiling was added

Above After Luke Lightfoot ceased work at Claydon some of the rooms were finished by Joseph Rose, Adam's favourite stuccoist. Rose created the saloon ceiling with its deep coffered coving, using classical motifs throughout his design. A massive Venetian window, that hallmark of Palladian design, its arch and entablatures supported by Corinthian columns, looks out over the grounds.

by Joseph Rose under Robinson's direction after Lightfoot's dismissal. It displays exquisite geometrical detail. The deep coving is of *trompe-l'œil* rosettes.

The library ceiling is again by Rose, but extraordinary winged brackets in the frieze are by Lightfoot. The bookcases and cupboards are full of old Verney bindings, many of them dilapidated. The room is charming, as is the view through the doors of the enfilade back to the North Hall. Classicism, to the modern eye often regarded as uniform and staid, is nowhere more variegated and alive.

Claydon's staircase is so precious that nobody is allowed to walk up it. The steps are of mahogany inlaid with box, ebony and ivory. No stair in England is its equal. The ironwork balusters are of equal delicacy, the swirling vegetation so finely wrought that it was said to 'sing' with passing movement when the stairs were in use. The dome above is a Lightfoot composition resting on Joseph Rose coving. To see these two masters of 18th-century decoration in such rivalry is a delight. In the Pink Parlour the panels tell the stories from Aesop's Fables.

All this is but an hors d'oeuvre. Upstairs is a sequence of rooms matching those downstairs. The Great Red Room is again by Lightfoot, notably the lions' heads of the window surrounds. The Paper Room contains Lightfoot's Rococo chimneypiece, composed of Chinese temples. Across a small museum is the bedroom used by Florence Nightingale, a Verney relative. Beyond is the so-called Gothic Room, so lighthearted and enjoyable as to merit the ultimate -k. Clusters of columns flank doors and windows. Even the window shutters are Gothick.

Finally we reach Lightfoot's masterpiece, among the most original works of 18th-century design anywhere. Sacheverell Sitwell awarded the Claydon Chinese Room his golden palm. Elaborate pagodas sit above the doorcases. Chinese faces peer from the woodwork. Swirling foliage interlaces scrolls, temples, bells and birds. The focus of the room is a large alcove, a grotto of fantastical woodcarving. The frame is like a proscenium revealing a divan. Inside is a relief of a Chinese tea ceremony, with two mandarins apparently waving at passers by.

None of this is kitsch, although it was seen as such by contemporaries. The design seems under control, always to a formal programme, an original work of genius. Claydon is poor in furniture and poorer in pictures, but no matter. It is a stunning monument to a master craftsman and to the waywardness of English taste.

Above The decoration of the Chinese Room is a testament to Luke Lightfoot's skills as a carver. Lightfoot combined Oriental motifs with swirling Rococo forms to create a perfect example of the chinoiserie style so popular in the 18th-century. His carvings run around the room, culminating in a magnificent canopied grotto. **Left** The inlaid staircase is Claydon's great treasure. Ears of wheat incorporated in the ironwork balusters are said to rustle when anyone climbs the stairs, in imitation of the real crop.

Cliveden shows what money can buy. Nowhere did Old Father Thames offer a finer view on his route across England. When Garibaldi stayed at Cliveden he declared the Thames at this point comparable with the mighty river prospects of South America. It was nature's gift to architecture in the Age of Landscape.

In 1666, on this bluff above Maidenhead, the 2nd Duke of Buckingham engineered a great platform and had William Winde build him a house to capture the view. The house was handed down to various owners and architects until the 2nd Duke of Sutherland and Sir Charles Barry decided to rebuild it after a fire in 1849. Barry based his design on that of the old house, including a medieval hall off-centre to the entrance, but the outward form is of an Italianate villa. Barry incorporated earlier wings by Thomas Archer, curving round the entrance courtyard. An ostentatious clock-tower was later built by Henry Clutton.

Cliveden was the sort of house that every rich man wanted but of which they soon tired – like Moor Park in Hertfordshire. The house passed from Sutherland to the Duke of Westminster. He sold it in 1893 to the American, William Waldorf Astor, who also bought Hever Castle, in Kent. The elderly Queen Victoria had enjoyed visiting the Sutherlands up river from Windsor and was mortified. She professed herself 'grieved to think of it falling into these hands'.

Fall was the wrong word. Lacking success as an American politician, Astor went to Rome as a diplomat in 1882 and acquired, said his grandson, 'a pattern of formalistic behaviour somewhere between that of a Roman emperor and his ideal of an English medieval baron'. He bought an entire balustrade from the Villa Borghese in Rome and set it beneath the house overlooking the parterre. He also bought the Rococo French dining room from the Château d'Asnières outside Paris.

In 1906, Astor went to live at Hever and gave Cliveden to his son, Waldorf, on the latter's marriage to the American beauty, Nancy Shaw. Where his father collected art, the 2nd Viscount collected people. To his weekends came Henry James, Kipling, Curzon, Balfour and Churchill. Bernard Shaw described a stay with Nancy Astor as like Sunday with a volcano. The guests later merged into the so-called Cliveden Set, advocates of the appeasement of Hitler's Germany.

Astor was an ardent conservationist, concerned to protect the rusticity of this reach of the Thames. His son, William, brought the house more notoriety when a cottage in the grounds was the setting for the Profumo affair in 1963.

'Nowhere did **Old Father Thames** offer a finer view on his **route across England.**'

Above The great hall at Cliveden is hung with tapestries celebrating the victory of the Duke of Marlborough at Blenheim. The Duke himself gave the tapestries to the Earl of Orkney, one of his most trusted generals and owner of Cliveden from 1696 to 1739. It was Lord Orkney who commissioned Thomas Archer's surviving wings, built in 1706.

Shortly afterwards the house was let to Stanford University. In 1985 it reopened as a luxury hotel but remains accessible. The magnificent terraced grounds were given by the 2nd Viscount to the National Trust and are open.

The exterior is pure Barry, an Italian palace on a hill, as grand as the vanished house he designed also for the Sutherlands at Trentham Park, in Staffordshire. The interiors are mostly rich 'neo-Barry', as refashioned for Astor in the 1890s. Rooms are panelled with fluted pilasters. Arches and windows are heavily draped. In the hall is a superb Italian Renaissance chimneypiece with, next to it, Singer Sargent's seductive portrait of Nancy Astor. The French Rococo dining room is as Madame de Pompadour left it and Astor acquired it. Upstairs rooms have been immaculately restored. To stay at Cliveden is expensive, but in a sense it always was.

Cliveden

Dorney court

⭐ ⭐ ⭐   A Tudor house, much changed and restored over time

At Dorney, 2 miles SE of Maidenhead; private house, open part year

Dorney is an island between the Thames and the far greater torrent of the M4/A4. The enclave of hamlet with ancient church, house, lane and meadows seems impossibly fragile. But Dorney still has its family, the Palmers, who acquired the house by marriage in the early 17th century and hold it to this day. They are tenacious.

The house is a challenge to any style historian. It is apparently a surviving late 15th-century structure. Gables sweep low over leaded windows, offset by soaring chimneys. Brick façades are carried on wooden beams, with bays thrusting and receding. Every feature of the garden is in proportion, shrub-clad walls yielding to paving and yew hedge, then to meadow and sheep. Yet Victorian prints of Dorney in the 1840s show a dull Georgian façade of three storeys with a pediment. What happened?

The answer is familiar to many old houses. A Tudor front was replaced by a Georgian façade in the 1730s which, in turn, was replaced by a Tudor one in the 1900s. How much of the garden façade of Dorney is old, how much imported and how much new is impossible to tell. The search for authenticity in the reinstatement was clearly thorough. The central gable is real Tudor from somewhere, but the overall effect more than a little 'Stockbroker Tudor'.

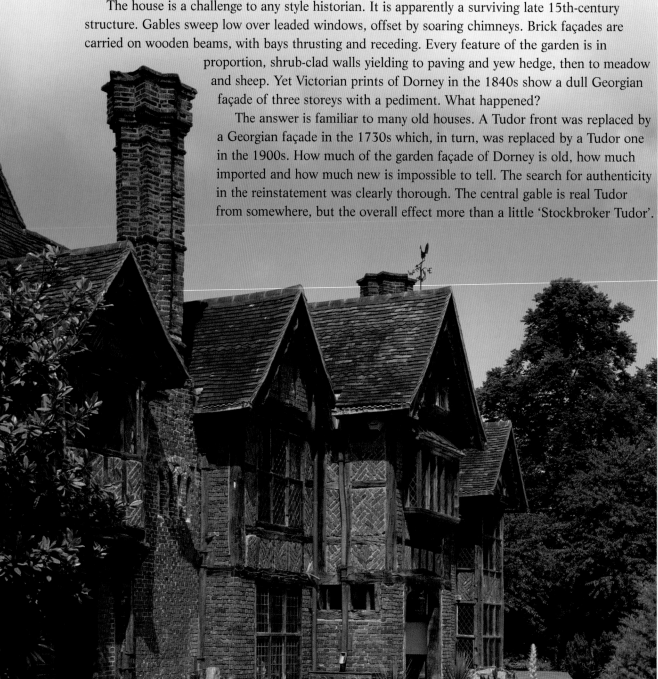

There is no arguing about the inside. The Tudor Great Hall survives, although much restored and magnificently displayed. A wide fireplace warms linenfold panelling. Persian rugs spread across a broad-boarded oak floor. In one corner stands a stone pineapple, in honour of the first such fruit grown in England at Dorney. Most rewarding of all are the 17th-century portraits that crowd the walls, mostly by Lely and Kneller, of thirteen generations of Palmers.

The plan of Dorney is as it always was, with service rooms and offices to one side of the Great Hall and family quarters to the other. Finest is the parlour, now drawing room, with polygonal window bays with pretty quarries in the glass. Here hangs a Jacobean needlework picture of Palmer triplets who were born on successive Sundays in 1489, and a portrait of Lady Ann Palmer on copper. Above the parlour is the Great Chamber under a barrel-vault ceiling. It contains a gigantic wooden canopied bed with posts like the legs of a Restoration courtier.

Downstairs on the other side of the hall is a small but sumptuous William-and-Mary style dining room with a painted wooden floor. It is a charming stylistic intrusion, Dutch classicism in a rough Tudor environment.

Fawley court

⭐ Restoration mansion with ceiling attributed to Gibbons

Near Henley-on-Thames, 6 miles W of Maidenhead; private house, currently for sale

Fawley claims to have been designed by Sir Christopher Wren. There is no evidence for this, but the custodian assured me that Wren is 'believed to have dropped by'. Nor is the beautiful saloon by Grinling Gibbons, although perhaps he was boating on the river at the time. In matters of 17th-century style, Wren and Gibbons are still synonyms for 'good English design', which is no bad thing.

The site of the old Restoration mansion is sandwiched between the Thames and the Marlow road with a canal leading from the house to the river bank. It was built in 1684 for William Freeman, sugar merchant, and extensively redecorated by James Wyatt at the end of the 18th century. After army occupation in the Second World War, Fawley became a Polish school of the Marian Fathers. Later it became a Polish museum, to offer 'a window of Polish culture onto the Western world'. Fawley Court became a religious house, open to the public as a wedding venue and as a retreat and conference centre. In 2008, the Marian Fathers made the decision to put the house on the market.

The interior is institutional but in a warm, Polish way. The hall has a black-and-white stone floor and is decorated with portraits of Polish kings. It leads directly into a double-cube saloon. This has red wallpaper and a superb Restoration ceiling. Its panels are filled with intricate naturalistic detail of birds and leaves in deep relief, as if they are about to take flight across the room. A stork holds a twig in its beak. Tiny animals run through thick vegetation. The attribution to Gibbons is understandable.

On the walls are excellent copies of Old Masters, including a Leonardo, a Giulio Romano and a Perugino. To the right of the saloon is the museum library, by James Wyatt in classical vein, with scagliola columns and icons on the walls.

Hartwell house

★★☆ Jacobean mansion transformed by notable Georgian architects

2 miles SW of Aylesbury; now a hotel

Hartwell is the best that can happen to a great house if there is no family to guard it. Hotel conversion can lead to death by fire regulation. Here, as at Cliveden, the atmosphere of a country weekend has been maintained. Reception is not intrusive. Books and pictures are appropriate. Grounds are immaculately maintained.

The original house was built c1600 by Sir Alexander Hampden, passing to his sister-in-law's family, the Lees (see Ditchley Park, page 125). In 1809, it won fame as home of the exiled Louis XVIII of France. A court of some 200 penniless French aristocrats descended on the place, camping in the rooms, keeping rabbits and vegetables on the roof and hanging washing everywhere. The alcoholic Queen Marie-Joséphine roamed the rooms objecting to the statuary. Louis's family stayed for five years, nearly wrecking the place, before returning to the throne in 1814 (and wrecking that).

'... furnishings and furniture
have all been chosen in keeping ...
This is a happy Renaissance.'

Later members of the Lee family found Hartwell impossible to sustain. It was let to Lord Leith and a rich American wife in 1914, but sold in 1938 for his own use by the ubiquitous conservationist, Ernest Cook, grandson of Thomas Cook and saviour of Montacute House, in Somerset. After the war, the house became a girls' post-school academy, in which guise I recall visiting it for a dance and finding it ripe with the smell of school food and decay. Soon afterwards the place caught fire. Cook's trustees finally leased it to hotelier Richard Broyd. He restored it with what *Country Life* called 'exemplary tact and sensitivity' before opening Hartwell as a Historic Houses Hotel in 1992. In 2008 the National Trust took over ownership; the hotel's profits will now benefit the charity.

The drive down to the house from the Aylesbury road is dramatic. A vista suddenly opens out onto an 18th-century landscape. On the left is a Gothic church ruin by Henry Keene of 1753, recently reroofed. It smiles as from a theatre box on the scene below. Ninety acres of avenues, lawns and architectural follies stretch to the River Thame. The lake bridge is formed from an arch of a former bridge at Kew.

The entrance front is E-plan and Jacobean. How it survived is a mystery, since the Lees were later to employ, successively, James Gibbs, Henry Keene and James Wyatt at Hartwell. Their interiors are dazzling. During the restoration of the house in the 1980s, a local architect, Eric Throssell, not only put back every recorded detail but, where none survived, created fresh ones in the style of his predecessors.

The Great Hall is of original Jacobean proportions but refashioned by Gibbs with plasterwork by Giovanni Bagutti and the Artari brothers. The same team worked for Gibbs and the Lees at Ditchley. The ceiling centrepiece depicts Genius rewriting History, an alarming concept. Beyond are the three main reception rooms along the east side, designed by Keene with Rococo plasterwork by Thomas Roberts of Oxford. The latter's work is outstanding (see Rousham, page 142). The staircase is a Gothick setting by Throssell for the old Jacobean stairs, adorned with statues painted to look like stone.

Beyond the staircase is a dramatic semi-circular vestibule inserted by Wyatt, rising the full height of the building. Along the south front are three new dining rooms created by Throssell. The biggest, loosely based on the dining room at 11 Downing Street, is in a Soane style. Another retains the columns of Keene's former chapel and a third is octagonal and tented. Colouring, furnishings and furniture have all been chosen in keeping with Hartwell's 18th-century period.

Left The vestibule at Hartwell is among the additions made to the house by James Wyatt (1747–1813). As an architect, he worked in both the classical and Gothick styles; his Gothick buildings were flamboyant but his classical designs owed much to the influence of the Greek revival. This influence can be seen in Wyatt's use of the more austere forms of architectural decoration to create an elegant semi-circular hall.

Hughenden manor

★★ Gothicized Georgian manor house and home of Victorian premier

1½ miles N of High Wycombe; National Trust, open part year

Hughenden is an ugly duckling. It was bought in haste for Benjamin Disraeli and his wife in 1848 on his selection as leader of the Conservative Party in the Commons, on the grounds that the party leader must have a country seat. The forty-four-year-old Disraeli was heavily in debt and the money was initially put up by his ally, Lord George Bentinck, and friends. Disraeli was MP for his 'beloved and beechy Bucks' and was happy to be near his father's home at Bradenham.

The house was a plain brick Georgian manor house, painted white, with a fine view south over the Hughenden valley. After twelve years of occupation, Disraeli commissioned the architect, E. B. Lamb, to embellish the outside and continue his earlier gothicizing of the interior. The redbrick refacing of the outside won the fiercest condemnation in Pevsner, 'excruciating, everything sharp, angular and aggressive ... window-heads indescribable'. It is hard to disagree. Disraeli planted assorted evergreens on the front lawn, perhaps to conceal the modesty of his residence. The National Trust has done the same, making it look like a market garden.

The interior is more endearing, although hardly less odd. Almost everything is in a heavy-handed Victorian Gothic, enlivened only by its intimate proportion. The hall ceilings are of stone, rib-vaulted, and strangely oppressive, the wall-hangings mostly dark. The library retains some feel of the Georgian original but the drawing room is emphatically Gothic. With the adjacent dining room, it well conveys the bourgeois solidity of Disraeli's England.

Benjamin Disraeli
1804–1881

As a young man, Disraeli first embarked on a literary career and wrote several novels that brought him some fame. He was, however, drawn to politics and became a Conservative MP in 1837. Prime Minister for the first time in 1868, Disraeli was to be the first, and as yet only, person of Jewish origin to hold the post – although baptized in 1817, he was descended from Italian Sephardic Jews. Disraeli came to be Queen Victoria's favourite PM and in 1876 he was responsible for making her Empress of India.

Above right Disraeli enjoyed a special relationship with Queen Victoria and her presence can still be felt in the dining room at Hughenden. Her portrait, which hangs between the windows, is a copy of an 1875 picture by Heinrich von Angeli at Buckingham Palace that the Queen had made specially for Disraeli in 1876. One dining-room chair is shorter than the others; when the Queen visited Hughenden in 1877, its legs were cut down to accommodate her tiny stature.

Upstairs, the modesty of the house becomes even more apparent. Disraeli's study is as he left it, a small room with desk and notepaper edged in black, used after the death of his wife, Mary Anne. Twelve years his senior, she said that 'Dizzy married me for money, but if he had the chance again he would marry me for love.' It is unpretentious in the extreme. To the rear is the Statesman's Room, recalling Disraeli's greatest foreign policy triumph, the Congress of Berlin of 1878. It displays the cherrywood fan signed by the delegates and presented to him in thanks for his diplomacy. On the staircase hangs the 'Gallery of Affection', pictures of Disraeli's political friends and associates. The house might be a cottage in the grounds of Pugin's House of Commons.

Nether Winchendon house

★ ★ Medieval house with Tudor and Gothick additions

At Nether Winchendon, 7 miles W of Aylesbury;
private house, open part year for tours only

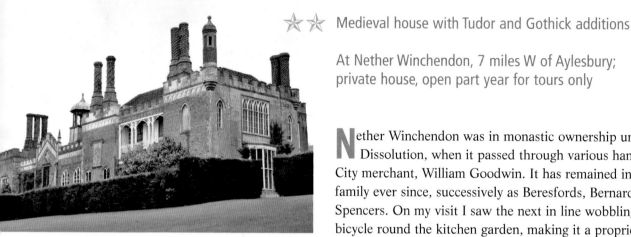

Nether Winchendon was in monastic ownership until the Dissolution, when it passed through various hands to a City merchant, William Goodwin. It has remained in that family ever since, successively as Beresfords, Bernards and Spencers. On my visit I saw the next in line wobbling on his bicycle round the kitchen garden, making it a proprietorial mess. This was strangely comforting.

The house is medieval, overlaid with Tudor, extended in Gothick and then left in peace – a typical English composition. The Tudor courtyard is fronted by an arched and battlemented screen. Two sides of the court beyond were given a Gothick front by Sir Scrope Bernard when he made the house his principal residence in the 18th century. On the far side, the house looks across lawns to the River Thame, which rises in winter to surround Nether Winchendon with an inland sea.

The entrance leads into a Regency hall, full of dark panelling, antique swords and looming portraits. Beyond lies the original Great Hall, converted into a dining room with a ribbed Gothick ceiling. It contains a 17th-century portrait of the Goodwin family, dominated by Lady Goodwin, her dead husbands relegated to pictures within the picture. The adjacent Justice Room replaced the old screens passage.

The glory of the house is its drawing room, a delightful work of Tudor Renaissance, c1530. The old linenfold panelling was painted white to celebrate the Restoration in 1660 and has not been stripped since. Rich carvings survive in the frieze and ceiling, dancing with arabesques, a mermaid and portraits of the owner. The windows carry armorial glass, and pictures of a butterfly and a fly.

The prize of this room is its tapestry, the only contemporary depiction of Henry VIII in this medium and said to be a close likeness. The king is flanked by Archbishop Cranmer and Lord Russell, briefly owner of Nether Winchendon. It was probably commissioned to celebrate Russell's creation as a Knight of the Garter in 1539. Garters adorn each border. Tumbling putti celebrate the majesty of the monarch and his status as head of the new English Church.

Above A 16th-century tapestry at Nether Winchendon shows John Russell standing to one side of Henry VIII. Russell served all the Tudor kings during his lifetime and was rewarded with many honours and extensive estates. Knighted by Henry VIII in 1539, he was granted several former monastic holdings by Edward VI – including Nether Winchendon and Woburn Abbey (see page 22). In 1550, Edward also made Russell 1st Earl of Bedford.

Olney: **Cowper's** house

⭐ Row of Jacobean houses, now a museum to two famous hymn writers and medieval lace

Market Place, Olney; museum, open part year

The poet and naturalist, William Cowper, occupied two adjacent Jacobean houses in Olney with his companion, a widow named Mary Unwin. Their servant occupied the other house with, so Cowper said, 'a thousand rats'. Cowper's house now has a kitchen on the ground floor with a waxwork of the servant working at her bobbins. She was paid £8 a year, considered above the local going rate. There is a rag-rug on the floor.

The rest of the house is a shrine to Cowper and his other local friend, John Newton, evangelical curate of Olney. Newton was a seafarer who was captured, enslaved and later became an anti-slavery campaigner. He and Cowper became a productive hymn-writing team in the 1770s and 1780s, their works including 'Amazing Grace' and 'How Sweet the Name of Jesus Sounds'. The house is filled with their portraits and memorabilia, including Cowper's pet hares and his smelling salts, the latter donated by Sir John Betjeman. Here too is the electric shock machine that the three residents appear to have used on each other to cure them of various ills.

The servant's house is a museum to the town's late-medieval staple, lace made by hand by refugees from the Low Countries. The garden that was such a feature of Cowper's writing has been re-created to the rear, with 18th-century plants. Its gardener corresponds on the subject of vegetables with the Gilbert White Museum in Selborne, Hampshire. On my visit, lavender and sunflowers were very much in evidence. Also restored is the summer-house in which Cowper worked. He called it his 'verse manufactury'.

Stoke park

★★ Georgian villa set in grounds landscaped by Capability Brown

At Stoke Poges, 2m N of Slough; now a golf club and hotel

Stoke Park is astonishing. It sits on the slopes of Burnham Beeches overlooking Slough, the M4 and the Thames as if it were a country club in the American Mid-West. The American parallel is not fanciful. The house was erected by John Penn, grandson of the founder of Pennsylvania, after 1789. Penn's father had already bought and rebuilt the old Stoke manor house and commissioned Capability Brown to lay out the grounds. His son returned from America, rich on annuities, and decided he needed something grander. He built away from the manor in the centre of the park, wishing perhaps to recall his house, called Solitude, on Pennsylvania's Schuykill River.

Penn's architect in 1789 was the little-known Robert Nasmith, but after his early death the work was handed to James Wyatt in 1795. Wyatt designed corner pavilions, a dome and colonnades. This was further amended when the house was acquired by Wilberforce Bryant, of Bryant and May's matches, in the 1880s. It became a golf club in 1908. The result is a bit like a wedding cake, especially the garden side, where the dome seems especially out of place. But the ensemble is

'I do not know how many **golf courses** are '**Capability Brown**'.'

undeniably majestic, in creamy white amid its green lawns. The courtyard entrance has a glassed-in portico, flanked by niches containing classical athletes and gladiators, fit sentinels for the royal game of golf.

The house is now a series of large reception rooms. At every turn there seems to be a scagliola screen or a classical panel, some surviving from Wyatt but most introduced by a Victorian owner, Henry Labouchère. A wide staircase in the central hall rises to a lantern under Wyatt's dome. Some traces of Labouchère's obsessive classicism remain in the statues and paintings. The former dining room has romantic murals by Thorvaldsen, of Love dominating the Four Elements, perhaps another golfing reference.

I do not know how many golf courses are 'Capability Brown'. But his work has been well adapted at Stoke. Hardly a bunker or a green is noticeable from the house. Instead, sweeps of parkland are carefully interrupted by trees. Each vista offers an obelisk, a church, a manor house, a lake or a clump of rhododendron. It is space well preserved in this overcrowded corner of outer London.

Stowe house

★ ★ ★ Architectural masterpiece designed, in part, by Vanbrugh, Kent and Adam

3 miles N of Buckingham; private house, open part year, grounds open all year

Stowe is a great English house in a noble landscape, symbol of the building mania that obsessed and often bankrupted the English aristocracy after the Restoration. The house and its grounds were first embellished by Richard Temple, one of Marlborough's soldiers and an ambitious Whig. He married a brewery heiress and from 1714 built in a frenzy until his death (as Lord Cobham) thirty-five years later. In the process, he created what were declared 'the finest rooms perhaps in Europe'.

His nephew and heir, Richard Grenville, Earl Temple, was said to be the richest man in England and continued the frenzy. The Temples of Stowe built temples at Stowe until they simply ran out of money. By the 1820s, they had risen to be Dukes of Buckingham and Chandos but titles brought no money. The richest family in England soon acquired the title of 'the greatest Debtors in the World'.

In 1827, the 1st Duke of Buckingham fled abroad. The 2nd Duke entertained Queen Victoria briefly and lavishly at Stowe in 1845, but with his creditors literally waiting outside for the monarch to depart. Three years later, the 'sale of the century' took forty days and scattered Stowe's contents to the winds.

Above left In Stowe's Marble Saloon, the design of the elliptical dome means that nearly every one of its 160 coffers is of a different shape and size. **Above right** The ceiling of the Music Room was part of Valdrè's work at Stowe and was completed shortly after 1781. The painted panels were restored in the 1960s and a copy of the central roundel, *The Dance of the Hours*, was made to replace the original, sold in 1922.

For a century Stowe was on and off the market. It was sold for use as a school in the 1920s but the sheer scale of the house and grounds have remained a problem ever since. The estate is now in the hands of the National Trust. The school buildings belong to a charity which is slowly restoring them. The interiors are predictably institutional.

The house is superbly positioned, with land falling away to north and south. Both from a distance and close to, it is a work of exquisite proportion. How this came to be is a miracle. For over a hundred years from 1677, architects as diverse as Vanbrugh, Kent, Leoni, Adam and the obscure Vincenzo Valdrè all lent a hand. Somehow, the cooks did not spoil the broth.

The north entrance front is centred on a bold, four-column portico probably by Vanbrugh and flanked by long quadrants of colonnades. The wings have recently been restored in lemon-coloured render, contrasting with the rich ochre of the portico. The entrance is almost as noble as Blenheim (see page 104). The south front, the rear, is more serene, mostly by Robert Adam. Here a more elegant Corinthian portico is flanked by the main *piano nobile*, balanced by pavilions with arched windows. The wide flight of 33 steps seems to invite nature in to share the joys of architecture. From these steps the vista stretches to a distant arch and on to the outskirts of Buckingham.

The interior of Stowe is a disappointment, never having recovered from the 1840s. Stone corridors echo with the sounds of school. Floors are uncarpeted. Walls have only a scattering of

Temple portraits. That said, the North Hall has a superb coved ceiling, covered in grisaille arabesques and rising to a central panel of Mars presenting a sword to Lord Cobham, painted by William Kent. Carved panels depict classical scenes. The adjacent Marble Saloon is the glory of the house. It dates from the 1770s and is based on the Pantheon, surrounded by 16 scagliola columns interspersed with niches (currently empty). Above is a plaster frieze of a sacrificial Roman procession, a Roman Elgin marbles.

The great reception rooms are blighted by decades of abuse. The dining room may again be feeding the children of the rich, but it looks and smells like an army mess hall. The reception rooms of the *piano nobile* retain their ceilings and chimneypieces – and their splendid view. On the walls are portraits by Ramsay, Beechey and John Jackson. The guidebook's pictures of these rooms in the 19th century make their appearance today the more tragic. Stowe, a monument to aristocratic hubris, is best regarded as conservation work in progress. At least it is still there.

Stowe Park: Gothic temple

A 'Temple of Liberty' created by James Gibbs in the grounds of Stowe House

3 miles N of Buckingham; National Trust, open all year

The English landscape can offer few more blissful scenes than a summer *fête champêtre* in the grounds of Stowe. Some time before acquiring the grounds in 1989, the National Trust held such an event. The evening was warm and an orchestra played Handel on the steps of the Temple of Concord and Victory. The Grecian Valley was filled with picnickers under lighted flares, like an army encamped before battle. It was a scene that would have gladdened the hearts of its creator, Lord Cobham.

Stowe's grounds were laid out successively by Charles Bridgeman, William Kent and Capability Brown, the latter beginning his career as head gardener here in 1741. The buildings in the grounds were by Vanbrugh and Gibbs. The Gothic Temple is the most lovable and most habitable of Stowe's twenty-five landscape structures. It is now tenanted by the Landmark Trust. It is also the only building not to reflect the prevailing classicism. Lord Cobham wrote above its door: 'I thank God that I am not a Roman'. A Whig radical, he regarded Gothic as the style of the liberal future. This 'Temple of Liberty' was to celebrate the freedoms of northern Europe against the stately tyrannies of Italy. It is ironic that by the end of the century, 'democratic' Greek, not Gothic, was the preferred style of revolution.

The Gothic Temple, built in 1741–2, sits by a clump of trees on the edge of Hawkwell Field, looking down on the Elysian Fields and on the lakes whose drainage taxed even Brown's skills. The pavilion was designed by James Gibbs and built of Midlands ironstone, a solid northern material preferred to the more effete, southern ashlar. The building is triangular, with towers crowned by lanterns at each angle. The style is free Perpendicular, castellated but with Early English windows.

Taplow court

★ ★   Jacobean house remodelled in the 18th and 19th centuries

At Taplow, 2 miles E of Maidenhead; private house, open part year

Taplow's golden age was Edwardian. Its owner, William Grenfell, was an Olympic sportsman and a Mayor of Maidenhead; he was still fencing for Britain in 1906 at the age of fifty. Two years later, as Lord Desborough, he organized the first Olympic Games to be held in Britain. The outbuildings include his old gymnasium. The house also entertained the late-Victorian aesthetic set known as 'The Souls' and was visited by Henry James, Oscar Wilde and Edith Wharton.

Tragedy soon followed. Two sons died in the Great War and a third in a car accident. The Desboroughs lived on at Taplow, housing evacuee schoolgirls during the Second World War. It then went into decline and saw decades of office use before being rescued by the present owners, the UK branch of Soka Gakkai International, a lay Buddhist society.

The original Jacobean house was converted by the Earls of Orkney to plans by Stiff Leadbetter in the 18th century. This version of Taplow Court was sold in 1852 to the Grenfells, who commissioned William Burn to return it to its previous Jacobean appearance. It is Burn's house that we see today. He raised its redbrick front by one storey; it is undeniably Jacobean but also gaunt and Victorian. The rear is quite different, French Gothic with flamboyant window tracery and a gratuitous tower. The best feature is the roofscape, of gaily twisted and decorated chimneys.

The focus of the interior is a remarkable 'Norman Hall' inserted by the Orkney heir, Thomas Hamilton, in the 1830s, before the arrival of Burn. It is of three storeys in the centre of the house, with arches and galleries, and is said to be modelled on Kirkwall Cathedral. The doors are beautifully decorated with panels of animals and foliage and appliqué woodwork in the tympanums. The dining room, ante-room and drawing room are virtually identical, with neo-Jacobean strapwork on the ceilings and marble fireplaces.

Waddesdon manor

✩✩✩✩ Palatial Rothschild mansion, built in the style of a French château

At Waddesdon, 5 miles NW of Aylesbury; National Trust, open part year

'... with a **view** across an **Italian garden** to a **fantasy** of **mansard roofs, dormers, chimneys, turrets** and **pinnacles.'**

Rothschild children were expected to marry Rothschild children. In 1865, Ferdinand de Rothschild of the Viennese branch married his cousin Evelina of the London branch. She died a year later in childbirth, but Ferdinand stayed in England and was joined as lifelong companion by his Viennese sister, Alice. In 1874 at the age of thirty-five, Ferdinand bought a large plot of hillside from the Duke of Marlborough in the Vale of Aylesbury. Here he realized what was to be his life's work, re-creating in the English countryside a French Renaissance chateau, furnished in the style of Louis XIV.

Waddesdon is an acquired taste, even as now restored to its original golden state. At the time of its construction, the English rich were ordering neo-Gothic or neo-Queen Anne. Leopold de Rothschild was content with neo-Tudor at Ascott House (see page 32). But Ferdinand wanted French, a style to which Victorian England had seldom taken kindly. That is not Waddesdon's fault. The house was to a Victorian Rothschild what a Grand Tour house must have seemed to a Burlingtonian. It merely substituted France for Italy.

Ferdinand died in 1898 and his sister in 1922. The house passed to their great-nephew, James, who was a Liberal MP and horse racing enthusiast. When he in turn died childless, the house and its immense collection of French art passed to the National Trust. It is now tenanted by the 4th Lord Rothschild.

The architect used by Ferdinand de Rothschild was the Frenchman, Hyppolyte Destailleur. He intended the house to be a *coup de théâtre*. Visitors ascended a winding drive planted with chestnuts and evergreens. Suddenly they burst onto a plateau with a view across an Italian garden to a fantasy of mansard roofs, dormers, chimneys, turrets and pinnacles. It is undoubtedly a *coup*, the word appropriately French.

The interior is a museum of furnishings and fittings. Waddesdon contains one of the finest private art and furniture collections in England, yet the National Trust keeps the rooms so dark, and visitors so distant, that it is hard to see the paintings at all clearly. Many are near invisible. The collection is almost entirely French, with imported panelling, tables, chairs, tapestries, carpets and desks. Not an inch is without ornament, yet nothing is cluttered. The taste is immaculate and of a piece.

The entrance leads into the east gallery, with two large Guardis of Venice. The chimneypiece is said to have come from a French mansion which had been turned into a post office. It must have been some post office. The breakfast room panels were from a banker's house in Paris. The dining room tapestries are 18th-century Beauvais, based on pictures by Boucher. The Sèvres table setting is so large and impressive as to defy cross-table conversation. In the Red Drawing Room are portraits by Reynolds and Gainsborough, including the latter's *Lady Sheffield*, and one of Waddesdon's many exquisite chests by the royal cabinet maker, Riesener. The Grey Drawing Room is from a house in Paris's rue de Varennes, with a Savonnerie embroidered screen.

Above left On the floor of the Red Drawing Room is a Savonnerie carpet, just one of several in Waddesdon's collection. Made in 1683 for Louis XIV, it features the head of Apollo at its centre, a symbol of Louis as the Sun King. On the walls hang portraits: to the right of the door is a 1782 Gainsborough portrait of the Prince of Wales, later George IV; reflected in the mirror is Gainsborough's *Lady Sheffield,* painted in 1785. On the ceiling is *The Apotheosis of Hercules, c*1725, by Dutch artist Jacob de Wit. **Above right** The walls of the dining room are lined with grey marble panels, inset with ornately framed mirrors. Once found in the gallery of the Hôtel de Villars, in the rue de Grenelle in Paris, these frames were probably carved by the sculptors Nicholas Pineau and Bernard in the 1730s. The spaces above the mirrors contain 18th-century reproductions of paintings by Italian masters; a copy of *A Sibyl* by Guido Reni is seen here.

Left Although small, the Green Boudoir was an important room – here Baron Ferdinand presented Queen Victoria with a fan on her visit to Waddesdon in 1890. As befitting the sitting room of the State bedroom suite, it was grandly decorated with more imported French treasures. The gilded *boiseries* – ornately carved panels – that line the walls came from a Parisian mansion. Baron Ferdinand, who acquired the panels in the 1880s, believed them to have come from the house of the Marechal-Duc du Richelieu but recent research has revealed that they originally lined a room in the Hôtel Dodun in the rue de Richelieu.

The west gallery in the front of house is equally sumptuous, but here one needs binoculars to see paintings by Watteau and a pedestal clock by Boulle. The tapestries in the small library are designed by Boucher. Next door is Baron Ferdinand's Room, containing a desk once owned by Beaumarchais, and a Riesener secretaire with lovely marquetry. Here are more English ladies by Reynolds and Gainsborough, well poised amid so much French finery.

The west wing culminates in the morning room, said to contain Waddesdon's finest paintings. Most are by Dutch masters, including de Hooch, Ruisdael, Cuyp and Dou. The black lacquered secretaire was acquired from an English family who were short of money but ashamed to part with it. Ferdinand bought it from them in secret, paying for a copy to be left with them lest their neighbours notice the loss.

The upstairs rooms at Waddesdon have been partly restored as bedrooms, partly as exhibition space. The former are a welcome touch of domesticity in this otherwise overwhelming house. The state bedroom and dressing room are dappled with Meissen and Bouchers. The Green Boudoir has panelling from a Paris house, with vanishing mirrors and much lacquer and gilt. The exhibition rooms display Rothschild Sèvres, Rothschild clothes and Rothschild wine.

West Wycombe park

★ ★ ★ Grand Tour mansion built by Hell-Fire Club founder

At West Wycombe, 3 miles W of High Wycombe; National Trust, open part year

West Wycombe is the home of the Hell-Fire Club and the creation of one man, Sir Francis Dashwood. Son of a wealthy merchant, Sir Francis lived from 1708 to 1781 and contrived to be Grand Tourist, rake, dilettante, Member of Parliament and a dreadful Chancellor of the Exchequer. He was also a popular and liberal country gentleman.

Dashwood's talents as a practical joker are perhaps better known. His exploits included attending a Vatican scourging ceremony with a horse whip, and masquerading in St Petersburg as the dead Charles XII of Sweden. But it was his visits to Italy, Greece and Asia Minor that informed his conversion of the house his father had built in the 1700s. Dashwood worked on West Wycombe from 1735 until the 1770s, with architects from the Society of Dilettanti circle, first John Donowell then Nicholas Revett. Once complete, West Wycombe remained unchanged, passing to the National Trust in 1943 but with the current baronet still in residence.

The exterior is perverse. It is porticoed on three sides, each one different and each asserting primacy. The National Trust makes visitors walk round all four to find the entrance, thus affording splendid views across the valley to the church and mausoleum on the hill beyond. Beneath the hill are the Hell-Fire Caves, where Dashwood's circle would meet and indulge in rituals possibly more lurid in legend than in fact. The valley is dotted with the customary features of a classical landscape – lakes, loggias, temples and lodges. The A40 and the village of West Wycombe, which cut across the scene, are remarkably invisible.

Right The stairs at West Wycombe are made of mahogany, inlaid with ebony and satinwood, and were probably crafted by a local cabinet maker. The staircase walls were painted with biblical and mythological scenes in around 1775 by Giuseppe Borgnis and were inspired by 16th-century frescoes at the Villa Farnesina in Rome. **Far right** The Tapestry Room is hung with early 18th-century examples of the art. Depicting peasant scenes taken from Teniers, they were presented to the 1st Duke of Marlborough – a distant relative of the Dashwoods – in celebration of his victories in the Low Countries. The tapestries are not in their original state; at some point in their history, they were altered to fit the size and fixtures of this particular room.

The interiors are an evocation of Dashwood's Mediterranean travels. They lack the serenity of Adam's interiors but are full of the motifs that immediately preceded him. Dashwood was mostly his own designer and the rooms are those of an eager tourist keen to show friends eye-popping pictures of his trips.

Entrance through the colonnade is directly into the hall, with its stairs screened by columns of scagliola marble. Beneath the stone floor is a hypocaust based on a Roman original found at Lincoln. The hall ceiling derives from Robert Wood's influential *Ruins of Palmyra*. The dining room beyond appears to be an extension of the hall, with the same floor and marbled walls and another 'Palmyra' ceiling. The

Tapestry Room, saloon and Red Drawing Room line the main front of the house, overlooking the view. The first has Brussels tapestries after Teniers, its wooden frieze and doorcase painted in *trompe-l'œil* and its ceiling Pompeian. The adjacent saloon is more spectacular. Here the ceiling is based on Raphael's *Story of Psyche*. Statues of van Dyck and Rubens grace the mantelpiece.

Most remarkable is the adjacent Blue Drawing Room, once used for dining and decorated accordingly. Bacchic revels cascade across the ceiling in celebration of the feast below. They are from the hand of Giuseppe Borgnis, an artist brought to England by Dashwood in 1752, and are based on Carracci's mural in the Palazzo Farnese in Rome – widely popular as a Georgian decorative model. The pier-glasses carry flowers and Ho-Ho birds. To James Lees-Milne, who worked for the National Trust in the house during the war, this was one of the most enjoyable rooms of its size and period in England, a Rococo response to Adam's statuesque ante-room at Syon House in London).

The final room, the Music Room, was intended as Dashwood's climax. The ceiling is again by Borgnis, based on Raphael's *Banquet of the Gods* at the Villa Farnesina. Other scenes are derived from Carracci and Reni. The walls are hung with Italian paintings of humans and gods in various stages of undress. The jewel of the room is the fireplace, like those in the study and Blue Drawing Room by Henry Cheere. Venus and Cupid cavort above piers dripping with leaves and cooing birds. The doorcases and pedestals are also by Cheere, an English signature on a thoroughly Italian house.

Hertford

shire

Hatfield House & Old Palace

Hertfordshire

Ashridge

★ Early 19th-century Gothic masterpiece by Wyatt and Wyatville

5 miles NW of Hemel Hempstead; private house, grounds open all year

Above The staircase hall at Ashridge rises up through the central tower. The entrance hall, with its hammerbeam roof, can be glimpsed through the arched stone screen, high above the stairs.

Ashridge lies at the centre of a large wooded estate owned by the National Trust on a limb of the Chilterns north of Berkhamsted. The house, a huge and romantic Gothic work by James Wyatt and his nephew, Sir Jeffry Wyatville, is now the home of a management college. Neither the house nor Repton's formal gardens are normally open to the public, but can be seen from the park. A guidebook can be purchased at reception, offering a discreet glimpse of the interior.

The house was an Augustinian monastery seized at the Dissolution and used, like Hatfield, for the safe keeping of royal children. It was from Ashridge that Elizabeth was sent to the Tower by her sister, Mary, in 1554. The old house passed to Elizabeth's Chancellor, Thomas Egerton, whose family were later Dukes of Bridgewater. It was they who demolished the old

building and began a new one with James Wyatt in 1808. The house was created in honour of the deceased 2nd Duke, promoter of England's canal network. The house passed to the Brownlow family of Belton House, Lincolnshire, became a Conservative Party training college in the 1930s, a wartime hospital and a finishing school before its present incarnation as a business college.

The house was built for show, like James Wyatt's now vanished Fonthill in Wiltshire. The main façade is to one side overlooking the garden. Its central feature is Wyatt's chapel, the steeple making the house seem like a complete village when seen from a distance. Turrets, towers and ranges of buildings sprawl on all sides. Facing the road is the entrance front, Tudor Gothic in silvery white stone. The entrance hall has a double hammerbeam roof with, guarding the second hall within, a stone screen with triple arched gallery.

Behind is the staircase hall, a thrilling medieval-style chamber rising to a high fan vault. A decorative wind vane is embedded in its central rose. The walls carry Gothic niches with effigies of figures from the history of the old monastery. The cantilevered stairs have iron balusters. These vast, interpenetrating spaces, new to English domestic architecture at the time, were made feasible by the great advances in heating technology.

The chapel has fan vaults and an oak organ case by Wyatville. As John Julius Norwich writes, 'architecture more unsuitable for the study of advanced business techniques could hardly be imagined'.

Brocket hall

★★ Home of the disreputable Lady
Caroline Lamb

2 miles W of Welwyn Garden City; now a hotel

Brocket Hall is a monument to aristocratic misbehaviour. The lady of the house, Lady Melbourne, was a mistress of the Prince Regent, who often came here to visit her and her son, the future Lord Melbourne, Queen Victoria's prime minister. Melbourne's wife was Lady Caroline Lamb, briefly mistress to Lord Byron. It was in the ballroom at Brocket that Lady Caroline is said to have been 'served up' naked in a giant tureen. Both Lord Melbourne and later Lord Palmerston lived and died at Brocket. After the current Lord Brocket fell foul of the authorities and spent some time at Her Majesty's pleasure, the house became a hotel, although it is still owned by the Brockets.

The building lies across a generous park of cedars and willows, with a spaciousness rare in confined Hertfordshire. The drive reaches its climax when a corner is turned and the house is seen in the distance, on an elevation overlooking a lake. The positioning is superb but, as often with mid-Georgian buildings, the exterior is disappointing. The architect was James Paine in 1760 and the proportion seems lumbering and top heavy. He always preferred an arresting roofline. From a distance, Brocket Hall might be an army staff college.

The more remarkable is Paine's interior, mostly decorated for the 1st Lord Melbourne who inherited in 1768. The staircase rises between balusters of a lively honeysuckle pattern and returns to a balcony beneath an arched and panelled ceiling. It is Paine's masterpiece. The main reception rooms retain their 18th-century decoration and some of the house's original paintings.

The saloon, now ballroom, was decorated by Paine for the 1st Lord Melbourne in a style worthy of his princely guests. It abandons all restraint, allegedly inspired by Adam's celebrated (and lost) Glass Drawing Room at Northumberland House in London. It seats fifty-four people, not including the occupant of a tureen. The coved ceiling is gilded and filled with painted panels, most by John Hamilton Mortimer. He is dismissed in the county's *Shell Guide* quaintly as 'a painter of the grotesque and horrible, dissolute, a cricketer'. On the wall is a Reynolds given to his mistress by the Prince Regent. Among the guest bedrooms are some decorated with his favourite chinoiserie.

Gorhambury hall

✦✦✦ Palladian mansion with impressive portico

2 miles W of St Albans; private house, open part year

Where would the Home Counties be without the tenacity of old landowners? The first Gorhambury, now a ruin, was built by Sir Nicholas Bacon, courtier under both Henry VIII and Elizabeth and father of Francis Bacon. The estate passed by marriage from the Bacons to the Grimstons, later Earls of Verulam, who hold it to this day. It was the 3rd Viscount who, in 1777, commissioned Sir Robert Taylor to build a new Palladian house at some distance from the old building.

The park lies sandwiched between the suburbs of St Albans and the hell of Hemel Hempstead. Taylor's house has a lofty Corinthian portico raised on a plinth, with a modest house attached behind it. This makes a tremendous show across the park, especially since its recent recladding in Portland stone. The house is mostly a casket for the family picture collection, including a so-called 'gallery of the great', of English monarchs and others. There is a run of Grimston portraits from the 15th century to the present day.

Above The crumbling remains of Old Gorhambury (now an English Heritage site) still stand in the grounds of the 18th-century Palladian house (below left). Built by Sir Nicholas Bacon in 1568 around two courtyards, Old Gorhambury merited two visits from Queen Elizabeth I. The house was partly demolished in the 1780s, when the new mansion was being built, and all that stands now is the two-storey porch and the Great Chamber.

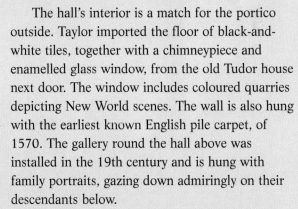

The hall's interior is a match for the portico outside. Taylor imported the floor of black-and-white tiles, together with a chimneypiece and enamelled glass window, from the old Tudor house next door. The window includes coloured quarries depicting New World scenes. The wall is also hung with the earliest known English pile carpet, of 1570. The gallery round the hall above was installed in the 19th century and is hung with family portraits, gazing down admiringly on their descendants below.

The dining room contains Jacobean portraits, including one by van Dyck, while the mantelpiece displays 18th-century bronzes of classical figures. In the ballroom are two startling Hilliards, one of the elderly Elizabeth I, so unappealing as to be surely a likeness. Essex is depicted in a more glamorous light. Everywhere are Bacons and Grimstons, in ruffs, doublets, ringlets, cloaks, stovepipe hats and swirling silks. The history of English costume is at Gorhambury.

The Yellow Drawing Room is dominated by a Grand Tour chimneypiece commissioned from Piranesi (another is in the library). Above it hangs a Reynolds conversation piece of the Grimston children. On the far wall is an extraordinary work, de Laszlo's portrait of the wife of the 4th Earl with her son. They are in classical pose and costume, but with unmistakably 20th-century faces.

Entering Hanbury Manor is like passing into Alice's Wonderland. Either we are suddenly very small or it is very big. The old house was called Poles and was Georgian. In 1800 it passed to Sampson Hanbury, the London brewer, whose family owned it until 1884. The house was then demolished and replaced by an 'earlier' building designed in 1890 by Sir Ernest George & Peto in a Jacobethan style. It is one of that firm's most extravagant creations, a Jacobean manor blown up to twice its normal scale.

Hanbury then had a sad history. In 1913 it was sold to a businessman, Henry King, who lost a son in the Great War and a daughter at the house when her beekeeping equipment caught fire. The family could not bear to stay. From 1923 to 1986 the house was a convent school. New wings and courts were added in 1930s Tudor. The place was converted into a Marriott hotel in 1996, but no amount of corporate design can obliterate George & Peto's monumental façade and reception rooms. Outside is a fine lawn and arboretum.

The exterior combines Jacobean and Renaissance themes. Redbrick chimneys rise above gables, each different in style and each larger than life. The interior is no less monumental. The Oak Hall has long Elizabethan windows above rich panelling. The library is panelled in mahogany and rosewood, with original bookcases and an astonishing Italian Renaissance fireplace. The dining room comes complete with barrel vault covered in the signs of the zodiac. Other rooms are equally grandiloquent. At the end of a corridor is the former convent chapel, now a banqueting room, with a stone reredos still in place.

Hanbury manor

Hatfield house

★★★★ Jacobean palace and home of great English statesmen throughout the centuries

Near Hatfield, 5 miles E of St Albans; private house, open part year

Hatfield is the epitome of early Stuart ostentation, a massive, overstated pile and beloved of Victorian imitators. From here, a cavalcade of Cecils has ridden forth to serve as statesmen, writers and controversialists. For four centuries, the English state has seemed unable to survive without the oversight of Cecils. Three Marquesses of Salisbury in a row were leaders of the House of Lords.

The house is next door to Henry VIII's old palace (see page 84). The new building was created by the hunchback 1st Earl of Salisbury, after James I had exchanged Hatfield Old Palace for Salisbury's Theobalds (which stood about 10 miles away to the south-east and was demolished in 1651). Today's Hatfield is thus Jacobean and prodigiously so. It sits in its sweeping park, surrounded by parterres and avenues, lakes and woods, defying the encircling suburbia of Hertfordshire. The enclave is hugely precious.

The house was built between 1607 and 1612. The plan is certainly Elizabethan, E-plan above a Renaissance loggia with classical frontispiece and brick wings. The designer was Robert Lyminge, who also created Blickling, in Norfolk, although the

'It sits in its sweeping park ... defying the encircling suburbia of Hertfordshire.'

frontispiece is attributed to Inigo Jones. The house has lost the surrounding terraces and statuary, but remains hugely imposing in its landscape. Visitors are able to see only the state rooms and then only in one direction. The experience is not so much of a tour round a great house as of a sustained *coup de théâtre*.

The principal *coup* is undoubtedly the Marble Hall, a glowing edifice rising above its marble chequerboard floor. The room was completed in 1612 and has not been altered since. The tables and benches were made for it. The colossal screen and minstrels' gallery carry their original carving, of cartouches, scallops and scrollwork panels heavy with heraldry and gilding. Few screens of the period tell of such inherited assurance.

Beneath the Brussels tapestries are portraits of the Tudor dynasty on whose favour Hatfield was built, the *Ermine Portrait* of Elizabeth I by Nicholas Hilliard and a portrait of Mary, Queen of Scots. The enigmatic *Rainbow Portrait* of Elizabeth, her dress covered in eyes and ears, her hand resting on the rainbow of peace, also hangs here. The room is like a theatre perpetually awaiting an audience.

The Grand Staircase was by the same hand as the hall's screen, a craftsman called John Bucke. The newel posts carry statues and heraldry, including one of the Stuart gardener, John Tradescant. The staircase ascends on a cloud of Cecil glory to the King James Drawing Room, the former Great Chamber. The ceiling is of white and gilt panels. A painted statue of James I adorns the marble

Above left The Grand Staircase at Hatfield is one of the finest examples of its kind. The oak balusters and newel posts are all elaborately carved. Even the gates on the first flight of stairs – designed to keep dogs out of the upstairs rooms – are highly decorated. **Above** The carved woodwork of the Marble Hall – the panelling, the screen, the gallery and ceiling – remains little changed since the carpenter, William Wode, and the carver, John Bucke, finished work in 1612. Even the benches and tables – for which the carpenter was paid £10 in 1611 – are original.

fireplace, standing lifesize but looking even larger and wonderfully pompous. The Long Gallery runs the length of the south front, its ceiling covered in gold leaf. Two great fireplaces face out across the room to gardens. These and the Long Gallery's sumptuous panels leave little room for pictures. A charming alcove, the North Gallery, looks down on the Marble Hall.

Beyond is the Winter Dining Room, fashioned from two rooms in the 19th century with a majestic Renaissance chimneypiece. On the walls are portraits of James I and Charles I by Mytens. The library completes the circuit. This is a dark room heavy with a marble fireplace. This frames an unusual mosaic portrait of the builder of the house, the 1st Earl of Salisbury, said to be a perfect likeness. The red leather furniture has been restored using dyed Nigerian goatskin.

The way out is through the Armoury, fashioned from what was once an open loggia. Polished breastplates and halberds are reflected in the shining marble floor. At one end, somewhat incongruous, is a Dutch organ supplied to the house as early as 1609. It should be playing a galliard as we depart.

Hatfield: Old Palace

⭐ Tudor royal palace, home of the children of Henry VIII

Near Hatfield, 5 miles E of St Albans; private house, open part year

'...darkly magnificent in the lee of the big house...

There are two Hatfields, adjacent but wholly different in history and character. The old palace was built by the Bishop of Ely in about 1485 and seized by the Crown on the Dissolution. It was used by Henry VIII to warehouse his children well away from the danger of court. Here the young Mary was said to have waved to him on a visit, after he had divorced her mother, Catherine of Aragon. Henry cruelly turned his head away. Edward and Elizabeth were also kept here for much of their young lives.

It was at Hatfield that Elizabeth endured virtual imprisonment during Mary's short reign. She enjoyed acting and singing, and even entertained her sister when the latter made a brief visit. It was in the park at Hatfield that she was told that she was queen, a scene repeated so often in films as to be beyond authentication. 'It is the Lord's doing,' she said, 'and it is marvellous in our eyes.' Her first council took place in 1558 in the Great Hall of the palace. It was here that she summoned her closest counsellor, William Cecil, Lord Burghley.

Elizabeth did not favour Hatfield as a palace, perhaps for its past associations with her unhappy youth. Her successor, James I, swapped it for the grander Theobalds, Hertfordshire home of Burghley's son, the 1st Earl of Salisbury. Salisbury demolished most of the old Hatfield palace when he built his own mansion next door, but he retained the hall range as stables.

This range now stands darkly magnificent in the lee of the big house, gazing across at it like a spinster aunt. It is one of the most extravagant brick buildings to survive from the Middle Ages. The expanse of 15th-century brickwork, laid in English bond, must have seemed sensationally rich when built. The windows are set high, like a clerestory, and run the length of the façade. The stub ends of the demolished side wings are now gabled chambers. The central porches on both fronts carry towers.

Inside, the hall roof now runs clear along the entire building. It is arched and with two tiers of wind braces. The Tudors removed the partitions from the kitchen side of the entrance to form one massive space for horses. It is a now a splendid venue for neo-Elizabethan banquets. The old palace courtyard is a knot garden, laid out with suitable Tudor plants by Lady Salisbury in 1984.

Knebworth house

★★★★ Victorian mansion of many turrets with J. G. Crace interiors

Near Knebworth, 3½ miles S of Stevenage; private house, open part year

Knebworth is a Victorian fantasy house, creation of the eccentric novelist and statesman, Edward Bulwer-Lytton, 1st Lord Lytton. He inherited the house in 1843 shortly after the break-up of his disastrous marriage to an Irish girl, Rosina Wheeler. The unhappy liaison had led Lytton's mother to cut off his income and force him into a voluminous writing career and then into public life. After their separation, Lytton and Rosina fought for forty years. He tried to incarcerate her in an asylum after she disrupted a political meeting at which he was speaking. She was released by public demand and wrote fierce novels and pamphlets attacking the subjugation of women. Ostracized by the family, Rosina became an icon of the suffragette movement.

Lyttons have lived at Knebworth since the 15th century, passing so often through the female line as to exhaust even the English talent for deed polls and triple-barrelling. Successive alterations to the house tended to be made by strong-minded women, including Bulwer-Lytton's domineering mother. Henry Lytton Cobbold is the latest owner struggling to keep the show on the road.

Below The Falkland Room at Knebworth is named after Rebecca, Viscountess Falkland, daughter of Sir Rowland Lytton (1615–74). The walls are decorated with hand-painted Chinese wallpaper, dating from the early 20th century, but it is the Chinese bridal bed, a traditional gift from the groom's parents, that dominates the room. The bed is made in different sections so that it could be taken apart and easily transported.

The house today is a memorial to Edward Bulwer-Lytton, 1st Baron Lytton. It was originally a Tudor courtyard mansion, much bashed throughout history. It became successively Jacobean, castellated Georgian and gothicized Victorian. It now looks like an oriental palace, with turrets, onion cupolas and protective griffons on pillars, a sort of Home Counties Brighton Pavilion. The building material is variously redbrick, pink wash, stone and render. Parts of the façades are well restored, parts creeper-clad and shabbily genteel, enhancing the picturesque effect.

The interior is in a rich variety of styles. It is mostly the work of the Victorian decorator, J. G. Crace, and Sir Edwin Lutyens, a Lytton relation. The entrance hall is by Lutyens, another of his whimsical variations on a classical theme. The adjacent banqueting hall has Palladian panelling attributed to Inigo Jones's pupil, John Webb. The raucous minstrels' gallery and ceiling are also Jacobean, but could hardly have less in common with Webb's classical severity. Lytton's friend, Charles Dickens, performed amateur theatricals in this room and Churchill painted it in the 1930s.

The downstairs dining parlour and library are relatively staid. The former is Jacobean in character, with 17th-century red-and-silver embroidered chairs and portraits of Lyttons, both Parliamentarian and Royalist. The library is almost demure, crowded with editions of Bulwer-Lytton's seventy published works and a treasured miniature of Mary, Queen of Scots. Over Lutyens' fireplace is an intense study of Lytton by G. F. Watts.

Upstairs matters are more riotous. The staircase is heavy with Nubian slaves and suits of armour. Everywhere are pictures of Lyttons. On the landing is Daniel Maclise's 1850 study of the author at his most romantic. Next to it is a sketch of the unhappy Rosina, who has now been reinstated as a celebrated figure in the family story.

Crace's two masterpieces at Knebworth are Bulwer-Lytton's study and the state drawing room. The study is furnished as the writer left it, richly panelled although not as rich as in his day. His long pipe rests on the chair. He described the pipe as 'that great soother and pleasant comforter ... blue devils fly before its honest breath'. Here too is the crystal ball into which he would gaze for hours in search of inspiration. The oval ante-room and state drawing room are remarkable interiors, the embodiment of Victorian Gothic romanticism. The theme of the ceiling, chimneypiece and stained glass is of the Lytton descent from the Tudors, with Henry VII in pride of place. A Maclise painting depicts Edward IV visiting Caxton's printing press, an iconic Pre-Raphaelite moment.

Knebworth has admirable bedrooms on show. Most magnificent is the Queen Elizabeth Room, supposedly slept in by the queen. The decoration is heavily Jacobean, with caryatids supporting the overmantel. On the wall is a curious picture of a nun, a monk and a baby. A painting of Diana the Huntress has been considered as possibly of the young Elizabeth.

Edward's son, Robert, rose to become Viceroy of India and 1st Earl of Lytton in the 1870s. An Indian exhibition is in the squash court. Giant rock concerts grace the grounds.

Letchworth:
296 Norton Way South

⭐ Shrine to the first suburban 'garden city'

Norton Way South, Letchworth Garden City; museum, open all year

Letchworth Garden City was intended as a Utopian heaven. The vision was that of the planner Ebenezer Howard in his book, *Tomorrow: the Peaceful Path to Real Reform*, published in 1898. The community was a suburban idyll of health and efficiency, co-education and a 'creative' curriculum. Cottagey houses and summer schools would stimulate a world of self-help, book-binding and sandal-making. A non-alcoholic pub, the Skittles Inn, served Cydrax and Bovril and was to be used for adult education. It would also act as a 'meeting place for striking workers'. Residents did not vote to admit a real pub until 1958.

While there was nothing new in garden suburbs or model communities – from Bedford Park to Port Sunlight – the idealism of Letchworth, founded in 1903, captured the enthusiasm of new socialist planners. It seemed a fit response to the overcrowding, smoke and disease of 19th-century inner cities and was soon imitated across the Home Counties and in France, Germany, Russia and Japan. Sadly, that idealism is now dissipated in a sprawl of commercial low-density suburbs, costly in infrastructure and hard to weld into working communities.

Cut out the idealism and the early exemplars have undoubted charm. Letchworth is proud of its pioneering past. No. 296 Norton Way South is the house where the architects, Barry Parker and Raymond Unwin, first put Howard's ideals into practice. The neighbourhood has the feel of a modest American suburb. The original offices were in a tiny thatched cottage set in a generous garden. After Raymond Unwin moved to Hampstead Garden Suburb, Barry Parker stayed behind and in 1937 built a small wing onto the office as a house for his family. They are linked by a small passage. A museum building has been added on the other side. Two original rooms survive in the Arts and Crafts style of the day.

At the far end is Parker's office, with a waxwork of Parker on the telephone at his desk, every inch the Edwardian architect. The room is beautifully furnished, with stained glass quarries in the windows, Arts and Crafts chairs, chests, bookcases and a copper fireplace. The family's old drawing room has been less successfully re-created as an Ebenezer Howard exhibition. The old man sits at his desk doodling on blotting paper, surrounded by architect's drawings. The garden outside was designed on the ideal of a 'tamed wildness', attributed to Gertrude Jekyll.

'The exterior is **extraordinarily** impressive.'

Moor park

✦✦✦ Mansion begun by Thornhill and reputedly finished by Leoni

2 miles SE of Rickmansworth; private house, open by arrangement

Somewhere north of Harrow the Rickmansworth housing estates retreat amid tumbling hills and hollows. Here in the early 18th century was an ideal spot for grand villas from which their owners could keep a weather eye on London. On the corner of a road, a sign points uphill across a golf course and into the woods.

To the schoolboy question, who made the money lost on the South Sea Bubble, the answer is Benjamin Styles, stock jobber and self-made man. But like many such men, he spent as fast as he made. He blew it all on a stately home. The Moor Park estate had already been owned by Cardinal Wolsey, then by the Earl of Bedford, the Duke of Monmouth and the Duchess of Buccleuch. Styles bought it in 1720 and proceeded to rebuild.

His first architect was, strangely, the painter, Sir James Thornhill, soon dismissed as too expensive and too old-fashioned. His style was for the Baroque and for historical and military decoration. By the 1720s, fashion was becoming lighter, with myths of Greece and Rome as mural themes. Thornhill is supposed to have been succeeded as architect at Moor Park by Giacomo Leoni, builder of Lyme Park in Cheshire.

The exterior is extraordinarily impressive. Partly because Moor Park lies in a hollow, the façade seems to shoot upwards like rockets from the ground, making it one of the most exciting houses close to London. The exterior is severely classical, yet still in the pre-Burlington Baroque tradition of Wren

Above When a visitor to Moor Park enters the Great Hall and looks up, the room appears to rise to an impressive dome; this is an illusion. The Rococo-style dome is a perfect example of *trompe-l'œil* painting. **Right** If the same visitor climbs to the first-floor gallery and looks up again, the illusion is lost and the painted ceiling now appears flat. Benjamin Styles originally commissioned Sir James Thornhill to decorate the Great Hall, including 'the Great Circle in the Ceiling', and had agreed a fee of £3,100. However, a dispute between patron and artist over monies paid and work done ended with Thornhill being dismissed and the commission being passed to two Italian artists, Francesco Sleter and Jacopo Amigoni. Both men had moved to England, Sleter in c1719 and Amigoni in c1730, to pursue lucrative careers decorating some of the grandest houses in the country; the paintings at Moor Park are among their finest works.

and Hawksmoor. The portico is stately, of four Corinthian columns rising to an enriched pediment. Pilasters on high bases decorate the walls, rusticated on the ground floor. The pediment cries out for statues, as at Lyme.

Inside, we can still see fragments of Thornhill the muralist. Moor Park vies with the Royal Naval Hospital, Greenwich, as a display of the heroic scene painting at the end of the Baroque era. But by now, the pomp and flattery of Greenwich and Kensington Palace were on the wane in favour of the finesse of William Kent and Giovanni Pellegrini, Thornhill's rival at St Paul's Cathedral. In 1728, Thornhill suffered the humiliation of being dismissed, not just as architect but as muralist, to be replaced by Francesco Sleter and Jacopo Amigoni.

The front door gives directly onto the Great Hall, probably gutted by Styles on dismissing Thornhill. It is a giant cube rising the full height of the building, galleried, sculpted and painted throughout. The plasterwork was by Giovanni Bagutti and the Artari brothers. Huge trophies fill the wall panels. The murals here are by Amigoni, classical myths replacing Thornhill's histories. Female figures lie languidly over the door pediments. To one side is a concealed staircase with more murals, again on classical themes by Amigoni and Sleter. From the upstairs gallery the *trompe-l'œil* of the ceiling is more apparent, beneath which are grisailles of gods and plaster effigies of classical dignitaries.

Beyond the Great Hall is the saloon. This voluptuous room celebrates the god Apollo in dark greens and blues. The god himself drives his chariot across the ceiling while the seasons adorn the walls. The artist is believed to have been Verrio, dating from the pre-Thornhill house. Along one side of the building runs the dining room, once a ballroom. A later owner had the ceiling panels painted by G. B. Cipriani.

The subsequent history of Moor Park was remarkable, even for a desirable villa near London. Styles blew his fortune and was followed as owner by Admiral Lord Anson, by an army provisioner, by a rich MP, by the Grosvenors, Dukes of Westminster, and finally by Lord Leverhulme; he formed Moor Park Golf Club in 1923. The house was headquarters of the Parachute Regiment in the Second World War and it was from here that the unhappy Battle of Arnhem was planned (a distinction also claimed by Stoke Rochford Hall in Lincolnshire). This is commemorated by an exhibition on the first floor.

Moor Park is a major London monument and should be better known. Its entrance front is spoilt by tarmac, car parking and adjacent tennis courts. It may be a golf club, but surely golfers have taste.

Shaw's Corner

At Ayot St Lawrence, 6 miles NE of St Albans; National Trust, open part year

'The villagers all thought he was a rum one, a very rum one.' George Bernard Shaw was forty-eight when he and his wife, Charlotte, went house hunting in the Hertfordshire countryside. They sought a place of peace and quiet, yet not too far from the bright lights. When they first saw the New Rectory in Ayot St Lawrence, they both disliked it – and therefore decided to buy it. Hating it suited Shaw's passion for work and his wife's passion for travel. Here they were happy in their celibate life together, with a staff of six and a distant relationship with the village.

Shaw would work ceaselessly in his garden retreat, dress formally for dinner and afterwards play the piano for his wife as she lay upstairs in her room. They lived here for four decades, until Charlotte died in 1943, and Shaw continued a further seven years until his own death. Shortly beforehand and aware of its likely fame, he wondered if the National Trust might be interested. He would not impose any conditions, but did not want it to be a dead museum. That is what it is. His bequest to the British Museum to reform English spelling met the same fate.

The house had been built in 1902 as a rectory but was too large for the local parson. It is an Edwardian villa set in a spacious garden and filled entirely with the belongings of the great man. The door knocker was donated by a friend with the inscription 'Man and Superman'. Inside the door is Shaw's collection of hats, including a tin-miner's helmet in which he chopped wood. The decor is late Arts and Crafts, moving to inter-war chintz. The study was Shaw's room, where he could sit either in the company of his friends or at least with pictures of them. The latter include Webb, Yeats, Barrie, Wells, the boxer Gene Tunney and many versions of Shaw himself.

'They sought a place of **peace and quiet** ...'

Left Shaw's Corner is full of evidence of the writer's life. In the garden is the rotating shed that could be turned to allow Shaw to catch the sun as he worked.
Above Pictures of Shaw and other writers (see text) hang in the study. Among the Shaw portraits is a caricature by Bernard Partridge from the cover of a magazine. **Below** Shaw's Oscar is on display in the drawing room. The author was unimpressed by the award and by his death in 1950 the statuette had become so severely tarnished that the first curator of Shaw's Corner used it as a doorstep.

The drawing room was Charlotte's room, but there is no escape even here. There is a bust of Shaw by Rodin and his Oscar for Best Screenplay (for *Pygmalion*) in 1938. In the dining room Shaw would spend up to three hours munching his vegetarian meals, believing that digestion should begin in the mouth. He would listen to music on the wireless in the evening, regularly calling the BBC if he heard a wrong note. The bedroom upstairs is as he left it, with his clothes still in the cupboard and shoes spotlessly shined. The kitchen displays the window through which Shaw's fan mail was passed by the postman each day.

Shaw's exercise was chopping wood and walking in the garden. At the bottom of the lawn behind a clump of trees is the hut to which he retreated if unwelcome visitors were hovering, to avoid the housekeeper having to lie by saying that he was 'out'. The hut is on a swivel enabling it to be turned to get the best light. It is laid with his notebooks and typewriter.

Woodhall park

⭐⭐ Georgian mansion with contemporary print room

At Watton-at-Stone, 4 miles N of Hertford; private house, open all year by arrangement

This is one of the sumptuous mansions built by Indian nabobs in the Home Counties, within easy reach of London. The nabob was Sir Thomas Rumbold of the East India Company. He had left for Bengal in 1777, telling Thomas Leverton, architect of Bedford Square, to build him a house and have it ready for his return.

We assume Rumbold was content. The magnificent house glows in cream-coloured brick on an eminence north of Hertford. Rumbold did not stay there long and the house passed to the Smith family (now Abel-Smith) who own it to this day. It is a prep school, accessible by appointment.

Leverton's house is firmly in the post-Adam style of Henry Holland and James Wyatt. It contains three sensational rooms, the saloon, staircase hall and print room, all somehow surviving seventy years of school use. The painting of the Etruscan saloon, now the entrance hall, is outstanding, more spare in its motifs than Adam and reminiscent of Wyatt's saloon in the style at Heaton Hall in Lancashire. Palm and anthemion leaves fall from the domed ceiling. The fireplace is of exquisite refinement, its medallions painted on canvas and stuck onto the painted marble.

'The magnificent house glows in cream-coloured brick ...'

Above The print room at Woodhall Park is a classic example of a form of interior decoration popular during the late 18th and early 19th centuries. It became highly fashionable to buy prints of various subjects and paste them directly onto the wall, arranged in groups. Print sellers also supplied the borders, frames, swags, wreaths and other motifs that were needed to complete a decorative scheme.

The staircase rises to a domed skylight past richly stuccoed walls. These become more ornamental the higher up they go, until they burst into half-moon fans at the top. The swags and drops are worthy of Joseph Rose, Adam's stuccoist, in white on sky-blue. Grisailles depict the four seasons and medallions the four continents. The staircase itself rises in a continuous sweep, with delightful iron balusters. On the first floor there are four real doors and four fake ones.

The print room of 1782 has recently been restored and is the finest of this rare genre in England. Whereas at Stratfield Saye (Hampshire), Rokeby Park (Durham) and Calke Abbey (Derbyshire), the prints are treated almost as wallpaper, here they are stuck onto the wall in a careful programme. Pictures of Rome and Florence take pride of place, with lesser pictures of landscape and famous people set symmetrically round them. They are divided by imitation pilasters and even have imitation hooks and wire. The house has a plan of the arrangement and a code to the print sources. It is a precious survival.

Oxford

shire

Stonor

Oxfordshire

Long alley almshouses

✫ Ancient example of sheltered housing

St Helen's Churchyard, Abingdon; private house, open by arrangement

Almshouses are today among the oldest inhabited buildings in England, almost all still in use for their original purpose. They offer 'sheltered' homes in the midst of their communities and are universally attractive. Of none is this truer than the enclave round St Helen's Church in Abingdon. Three sides of the churchyard are flanked by almshouses, turning what is often a bleak civic space into a place of delight. There is hardly a churchyard in England that could not be improved by some discreet building in this way.

The citizens of 17th-century Abingdon seem to have enjoyed a burst of competitive welfare. This group comprises Long Alley, Twitty's, Brick Alley and, at some distance, Tomkin's Almshouses. Each dates from the 17th and early 18th centuries. The oldest and most remarkable is Long Alley. It was founded as St Helen's Hospital in 1446 but was suppressed in 1546. Like many such charitable institutions it was swiftly refounded as Christ's Hospital in 1553. It had thirteen occupants and is still in use.

The dominant feature of Long Alley is its length. An immense tiled roof conceals a pentice or cloister beneath, sheltered by a continuous wood-mullioned screen. This is punctuated by a central porch and two lesser porches of 1605. The walls between the rooms' doors carry admonitory biblical texts. There is nothing else like this in England. A charming William-and-Mary lantern rises above the central hall.

When inaccessible, the hall can be glimpsed through its rear windows. It is an antique chamber full of ancient desks and tables, still furnished with quill pens. Dark portraits of early patrons gaze down from the walls. There is more comfort in these places than in a hundred National Health homes.

Merchant's house

⭐ Medieval town house with Tudor murals

26 & 26A East St Helens Street, Abingdon; private house, open by arrangement

East St Helens leads from Abingdon Market to the parish church in a graceful curve, each façade an instrument in the urban orchestra. Streets of such completeness are rare in England. The whole is so enjoyable that a casual visitor might miss Nos. 26 and 26A, owned by the Oxford Preservation Trust. They are formed from the ghost of a merchant's hall house of *c*1430. Two cross-wings with gables to the street flank a central hall, of which the lower part was wrecked when the Victorians drove a carriageway through it.

What survives are two houses and a bridge. The left-hand wing is slightly grander, presumably the old solar wing, and is private. The right-hand wing was converted into living rooms in the 16th century and is open by appointment. Either side of its gable is a trefoiled window. The windows on the ground floor are shuttered and picturesque.

The chief feature of the house is its interior decoration. In the downstairs parlour is a fireplace with medieval quatrefoils, while upstairs is another with a Gothic frieze of trefoils. These fireplaces were possibly imported from a dissolved monastery, as found in houses all over England in the 16th century. They made chimneys available to people other than the rich.

More extraordinary are the painted walls, mostly on the stairwell. Dating from the mid-16th century, these take the form of vertical bands of red and white, entirely covered in semi-abstract fronds and flowers. An identical pattern is repeated on walls and beams throughout the house, as if in mass production. A Jacobean doublet found during restoration is on view in a case downstairs.

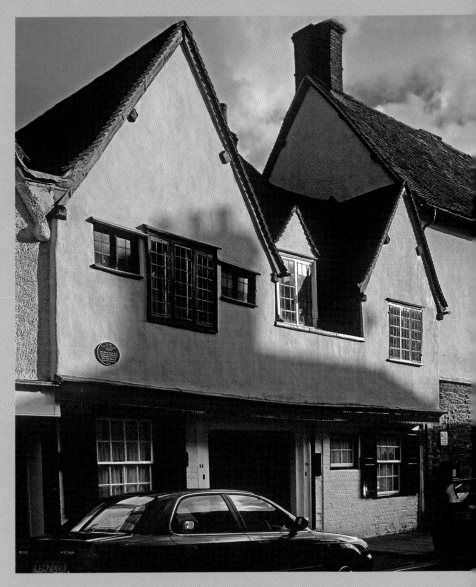

Ardington

⭐ An early Georgian house, in English Baroque style

At Ardington, 2½ miles E of Wantage; private house, open part year

The house lies on the edge of a formerly Berkshire village overlooking a park and lake. It is described in Pevsner as a 'swagger' house and even Vanbrughian. The property, owned by the Baring family, was built in 1720 when English Baroque was still in vogue. It is solid and rectangular, with sheltering cedars and a pretty pavilion to one side.

Both front and rear elevations have pedimented centre bays. In the pediments are effusive carvings round coats of arms. The door frames are rusticated. The materials add to the artfulness of the façade, pale grey bricks with red bricks for the window dressings. Ardington is a serious work of architecture, a memory of the era of Wren.

The interior is unexciting apart from the hall. This leads enticingly towards the double staircase which fills its far end, an extravagant use of space. The two arms rise separately, then turn to rush towards each other and meet out of sight. The effect is strangely erotic.

The dining room is finely panelled with fluted pilasters and Rococo ceiling plasterwork. This has been crudely picked out in white on a black background, as in a night club. On the walls are generations of Barings.

Ashdown house

★★★ A Restoration house, built as a retreat for the Winter Queen

7½ miles E of Swindon; National Trust, open part year

Sacheverell Sitwell gazed on Ashdown and declared it a Danish *slott*. It should be a backdrop for 'Swan Lake', he said, with cygnets dancing across its façade on stage machinery. The house is the jewel of the Vale of the White Horse, standing alone and beautiful in a fold of the Downs above Lambourn.

The Restoration 1st Earl of Craven was a devoted admirer of Charles I's sister, Elizabeth, wife of the Elector Palatine. She was married in 1613 and became Queen of Bohemia for one winter in 1619, before her husband's defeat in war. She was known ever after as the Winter Queen. Craven was an infatuated soldier of fortune who followed the Queen and her cause round Europe, financing her family squabbles and rescuing her from debt during the English Civil War. His letters to her contain no word of love, only utter devotion. Her letters to him are to 'my little mad mylord'. He won none of the jovial affection she bestowed, for instance, on another admirer, Lord Carlisle. He was greeted with, 'thou ugly, filthy camel's face'.

Craven worshipped the Queen all her life. He is said to have built, or converted, both Hamstead Marshall (demolished) in Berkshire and Combe Abbey in Warwickshire for her. Ashdown House was offered to her as a refuge from the Plague. She never came, ironically dying of the disease in 1662. She left Craven only a collection of portraits and some antlers. He never married and lived with these mementoes for another 35 years.

The house, empty and semi-derelict after wartime military abuse, was handed to the National Trust by Cornelia, Lady Craven in 1956. It stands, a perfect cube, beneath a steep roof with dormers. On top of the roof is a belvedere platform with balustrade. Each façade is the same. The walls are of chalk dressed with stone, shimmering silver in a low sunlight. In front of the house stand two detached pavilions with double-storey dormers. Round them roll meadows and hills, a superb setting.

Ashdown is attributed to the group of Restoration architects associated with Roger Pratt. William Winde, who worked for Craven elsewhere, is personally credited with Ashdown. There are traces of Dutch and French influence, characteristic of the Restoration. This must be appreciated outside.

The interior is not grand and the principal rooms are tenanted. Visitors see only the dramatic staircase leading to the belvedere on the roof. Its bulbous balusters rise on massive newel posts the full height of the house. Ashdown's treasures line the walls, the 17th-century portraits bequeathed to Craven by the Winter Queen. They are by Dobson, Miereveldt and van Honthorst and form a splendid progression, in tune with the spirit of the place.

Blenheim palace

★★★★☆ Vanbrugh's monument to British victory
and Marlborough's reward

At Woodstock, 8 miles NW of Oxford; private house,
open part year

Blenheim brooks no argument. It was primarily intended not
as a home but as a monument, symbol of British pride at
stemming French expansion in Europe. The moment of victory
was the Battle of Blenheim in 1704. The glory was thus
awarded to the nation and Queen Anne, as well as
Marlborough. Vanbrugh was chosen as its
architect in preference to Wren. Vanbrugh designed a building to shout. Blenheim
is an army lined up for battle. It is most un-English.

More English were the horrors of its construction. The manor of Woodstock
was granted to Marlborough by Queen Anne at a time when she and his
Duchess were intimates. Building began in 1705 with a labour force of
1,500, the bills met by the Treasury against a massive budget of
£240,000. By 1710, the friendship of the Queen and Sarah, Duchess
of Marlborough, had collapsed and Marlborough was out of
favour. Building at Blenheim ceased. The grant was almost spent
but work was anything but finished.

Six years later, the Duke resumed Blenheim at his own expense.
Vanbrugh stormed off after a row with the Duchess, and Grinling
Gibbons left as well. Vanbrugh's assistant, Hawksmoor, also departed,
leaving local masons in charge. The place was not habitable until
1719, by when the miserable Duchess was dubbing it the nation's
'monument of ingratitude'. When Vanbrugh tried to see his handiwork
later in life, the gatekeeper was told to refuse him entry.

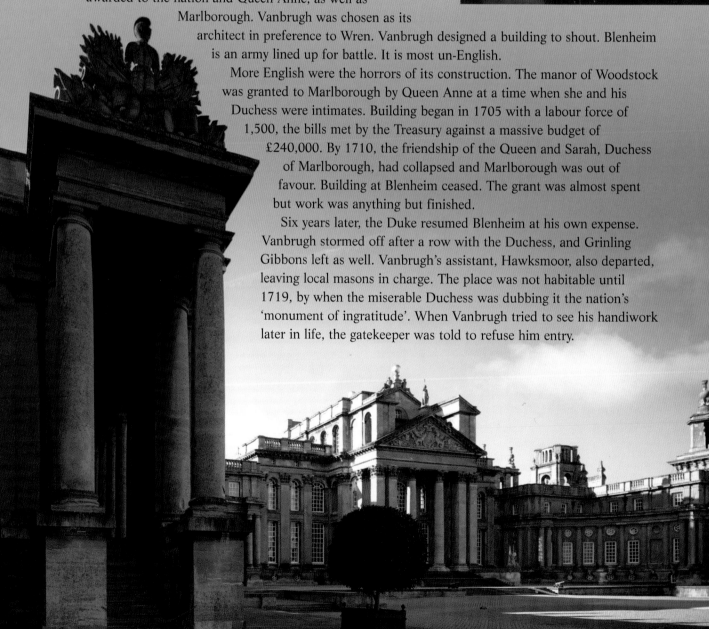

Left A portrait by Johann Closterman of John Churchill, 1st Duke of Marlborough (1650–1722), that hangs in the green writing room at Blenheim. **Below** The second state room is one of three interconnecting rooms that form an elegant enfilade between the saloon and long library. The tapestries that hang here celebrate Marlborough's victory over the French at Bouchain in 1711 and are part of a series that the Duke himself commissioned to commemorate his military campaigns. They were the work of Flemish weaver, Judocus de Vos, after designs by Lambert de Hondt.

Blenheim has always been as a giant among buildings, a true palace. George III admitted on seeing it that 'we have nothing to equal this'. The place is no less grand today. The grounds are the masterpiece of Capability Brown in the 1760s, long after both Vanbrugh and the Duke had departed. The drive from Woodstock to the side entrance and the axis from the forecourt out across the lake seem integral to the genius of the place. They are creations of Brown not Vanbrugh. Yet from every angle, Vanbrugh's great façade dominates the scene. It is a structure of receding planes, colonnades, towers and finials, seeming to sprout from its plateau. It is the truest manifestation of English Baroque.

Above The ceiling of the Great Hall was painted by Sir James Thornhill in 1716 and shows the victorious Duke of Marlborough kneeling before the figure of Britannia, presenting her with the battle plan of Blenheim. **Right** Thornhill was meant to have painted the saloon too, but he fell out with the Duchess of Marlborough over his fees for the Great Hall and the French artist, Louis Laguerre, was commissioned in his place. Laguerre painted a *trompe l'œil* colonnade around the walls and filled the space with figures, many of them portraits of Marlborough's friends and associates.

Entrance is through the stables courtyard. Mighty gates reveal range upon range of offices and apartments. The main front is thus approached from the side, also a Baroque effect. Statues and trophies crowd the roofline. A flight of steps leads to the central portico. Visitors should ideally arrive by chariot.

The Great Hall maintains the splendour of the façade. Clad entirely of stone, it rises the full height of the central block to a lantern painted by Thornhill. A giant arch containing a balcony frames the entrance to the saloon behind. The coat of arms over the door is by Gibbons. Busts, trophies, banners, everything declares the splendour of the Marlboroughs. Even the brass locks to the front door are copies of those on 'the gates of Warsaw'.

'Busts, trophies, banners, everything declares the splendour of the Marlboroughs.'

Above Vanbrugh originally intended the Long Library to be a picture gallery. The room, some 180 feet long, was one of the last to be finished and was completed following instructions Nicholas Hawksmoor had left behind after he and Vanbrugh stopped work at Blenheim. At the northern end of the room is a massive Willis organ; installed by the 8th Duke in 1891, the instrument once stood in the central bay.

Right Vanbrugh's palace demanded a suitably grand approach and the architect persuaded Marlborough to accept his design for an impressive arcaded bridge crossing the River Glyme in front of Blenheim's main façade. Soon after the bridge was finished, without Vanbrugh's planned arcade, the river was channelled into a canal, that ran under the central arch and into a formal pool. Later in the 18th century, Capability Brown dammed the Glyme and created the lake which the bridge spans today.

From this point onwards, I find Blenheim starts to deflate. Visitors are required to pass through a tired Winston Churchill exhibition – he was born in the house – before seeing the house. The public rooms run along the rear of the building in a continuous, frankly tedious enfilade. Three drawing rooms culminate in the saloon, followed by three state rooms. They seem interchangeable, hung with Brussels tapestries depicting scenes from Marlborough's campaigns, or with portraits of contemporary dignitaries. The saloon is entirely painted by Laguerre in *trompe-l'œil*, the only decoration in the room.

More delightful are the surprises. These include a charming Reynolds in the Green Drawing Room of the 4th Duchess dandling a baby; a Sargent in the Red Drawing Room of the 9th Duke and his Vanderbilt wife, epitome of Edwardian swagger; and Boulle chests in the Third State Room. The three great doorways in the saloon were undertaken by Gibbons before he walked away from the job. The two-headed eagles were granted to Marlborough as a prince of the Holy Roman Empire.

At the end of the enfilade one can turn and wonder at its sheer scale. The doors are so perfectly aligned that it is said daylight can be seen through all the keyholes. The Long Library is by Vanbrugh, but its remarkable central doorway, an arch beneath a scroll flanked by columns, is by Hawksmoor. The present Duke and his family still occupy apartments at the rear of the building. Blenheim is probably more manageable today than ever in its troubled history.

'Blenheim has always been as a giant among buildings, a true palace.'

Broughton castle

 ★★★★☆ Elizabethan opulence round a medieval core

At Broughton, 3 miles SW of Banbury; private house, open part year

Broughton is Hogarth's 'The Roast Beef of Olde England' in architectural form. It survives from the Middle Ages and is still inhabited by its founding family. In 1448, William Fiennes, 2nd Baron Saye and Sele, married a descendant of the owner, William of Wykeham. A century later, under Elizabeth I, the Fiennes family modernized Wykeham's house. They patted the last stone into place, pronounced it magnificent and have seen no reason to alter it since. Broughton is the English house at its first apogee in the late 16th century, a place of great chambers and cosy parlours, attics and knot gardens.

The Fiennes were comfortable but never rich. They seem to have treated politics as a distant evil and the Renaissance as a passing fad. The upstart 18th and 19th centuries were virtually ignored at Broughton. Lord and Lady Saye and Sele remain hugely proud of their house and display it with panache. Unable to afford a new standard, they repaint the old flag each summer. His lordship was asked by an awestruck Arab, 'You must need many wives to run this place.' He shamefacedly admitted to 'three in one'.

When built at the start of the 14th century, Broughton consisted of a Great Hall and chapel, with medieval solar and undercroft added later. These remain its core today. The house sits at the far side of a walled enclosure with a moat, and is reached through a gatehouse over a bridge. It was a defended manor rather than a castle, a Great Hall with Tudor chambers extending in a series of wings and towers to the sides and rear.

Despite its Elizabethan façade, the Great Hall is a bare, medieval chamber lined with weapons and armour. The big windows, fireplace and 18th-century ceiling are later insertions. Those confused

'Broughton is the **English house** at its **first apogee** ...'

Below When the Fiennes family renovated Broughton at the end of the 16th century they transformed the Great Hall by replacing the narrow Gothic windows with the present wider ones and by plastering over the ceiling and walls. The plasterwork pendant ceiling was added in the 1760s. In 1900, the walls were stripped back to reveal the original 14th-century stonework; the 18th-century pendant ceiling was left in place. **Right** The 16th-century rebuilding of Broughton began in 1554 and the chimneypiece in the King's Chamber dates from this time. It is believed to have been very similar to chimneypieces at Henry VIII's Nonsuch Palace, now lost. The room has played host to two kings; James I stayed here in 1604, and Edward VII in 1901.

by the complexities of the Twistleton, Wykeham and Fiennes families can view them artistically set out in a family tree on the wall. There was no Cavalier romance to Broughton. The Fiennes were Parliamentarians and proud of it.

The medieval house is to the left of the Great Hall. Passages with groined vaults lead to an undercroft. The vaults carry carved corbel heads, including green men, rare in domestic architecture at this date. The undercroft is now a dining room, with 'stitched' double linenfold panelling. An early depiction of the house has been carved in one corner. The house retains its 14th-century chapel.

Upstairs, cold medieval stone changes to Elizabethan warmth. A classical portal to the upper gallery announces Broughton's brief recognition of the 18th century. The gallery was inserted above the Great Hall by the Elizabethans, and decorated with thin Gothick pilasters in the 1760s. The wallpaper is modern, a bold flaming orange. Busts by Rysbrack of Ben Jonson and Inigo Jones stand at either end. The gallery has a portrait of the 17th-century William Fiennes, who fought for Parliament, opposed Charles I's execution and was duly pardoned by Charles II. His apt nickname was 'Old Subtlety'.

'... a place of **great chambers**
and **cosy parlours**...'

Two bedrooms lead off the gallery, both with remarkable fittings. Queen Anne's Room, named after Anne of Denmark, has a classical fireplace of the 1550s, with Artisan Mannerist capitals and entablature. The chimneypiece in the adjacent King's Chamber is a work of national importance. The plaster overmantel is attributed to Italian craftsmen copying work at Fontainebleau. Dryads dance round a sacred oak in a scene from Ovid. They are held in a roundel by two naked boys, framed by a Roman soldier to one side and a female figure the other. The work is Continental and sophisticated, strangely out of place in beefy Broughton. The walls of the King's Chamber have Chinese paper and a bold modern bed in oriental style.

At the west end of this range is the Great Parlour, completed as the climax of the Elizabethan rebuilding in 1599. The ceiling is of intricate geometrical plasterwork, its outline decorated with

Far left The plasterwork ceiling of the Great Parlour bears the date 1599; this was when Sir Richard Fiennes, 7th Lord Saye and Sele, completed the work begun by his father more than forty years earlier. Broughton suffered a slight decline in the 18th and early 19th centuries and by the 1850s the 16th Lord Saye and Sele needed to carry out some renovations. The doors and wainscoting of the Great Parlour date from this time, as does the imitation leather wallpaper.

Left The Oak Room is on the ground floor of Broughton's Tudor wing and was built over the site of the medieval kitchens. It has an elaborate internal porch that is believed to have been moved here from its original position in the Great Parlour, above the Oak Room. On the tall cartouche above the doorway is carved the motto *Quod olim fuit meminisse minime iuvat*, which translates as 'There is no pleasure in the memory of the past.'

leaves and birds and with pendants adorned with cherubs. Panels carry the family coat of arms. The wallpaper is Victorian. In an upstairs tower is the so-called Council Chamber, where Parliamentarian plotters, including Pym, Vane and Hampden, gathered under cover of the Providence Island Company in a 'room with no ears'. It has windows on all sides.

Beneath the Great Parlour is the Oak Room, once the dining room and now the most opulent of Broughton's reception rooms. The panelling is superb, divided by gentle fluted pilasters. High alcoves with bay windows look out over the garden. A magnificent internal porch shields the main door. Its Latin inscription proclaims that the past is best forgotten, a maxim much favoured by former Parliamentarians at the Restoration. The theme is repeated in a picture over the mantelpiece celebrating Charles II embarking for England from Holland. 'Old Subtlety' was still at work.

Buscot old parsonage

★ William-and-Mary house by the Thames

At Buscot, 9 miles NE of Swindon; National Trust, open part year by arrangement

The group of Buscot church and parsonage is the Thames-side dream of every American visitor. The last Stewkley owner was a bachelor who disliked his family and wanted at all costs to stop any relative inheriting the property. On his death in the 1960s, he left it to the National Trust requiring it to be tenanted only by an American artist or writer. This did not happen at first, the house going to an English woman, Diana Phipps. It has since passed to an American with an artist wife. The house is crammed with pictures and furniture in a delightful Anglo-American jumble of styles.

The exterior is unaltered William-and-Mary of 1701. A simple stone box of three bays by five is enlivened by a steep hipped roof, generous windows and Cotswold tiles. A massive wisteria gives it a warm cloak. The front door is at the top of a Baroque flourish of steps and the rear of the house opens onto an extensive garden of walls and lawns, merging into the surrounding Thames water meadow.

The interior has taken on the character of its tenants. The small entrance hall is entirely decorated with wild flowers painted onto the wood panelling. Twentieth-century ingenuity creates the effect of 18th-century gentility. One of the reception rooms is adorned with Diana Phipps's batik wall hangings. The upstairs dining room has a Chinese canopy hanging above the table. The wall colours were carefully chosen from 18th-century paint samples obtained from colonial Williamsburg, a fitting compliment from the New World to the old.

Buscot park

★ ★ ★ Georgian house with fine picture collection

Near Buscot, 8½ miles NE of Swindon; National Trust, open part year

The star of Buscot Park shines in its saloon, Burne-Jones' exquisite paintings of the *Legend of the Briar Rose*. When first exhibited at Agnews in 1890, the series caused a public sensation. Crowds packed Bond Street and 'enthusiasm amounted to ecstasy,' said one reviewer. The work was bought by Lord Faringdon who asked the artist to design a gilt surround as a setting. The result is one of the finest Pre-Raphaelite rooms in England. On a summer's day with the scent of flowers in the air, these languid sleepers amid so much green and gold act are truly soporific.

Buscot is a classic Georgian house enlivened by the eccentricity of its owners. Built in the 1780s, it was bought in 1889 by a City financier, Alexander Henderson, later Lord Faringdon, and filled with his collection of Old Masters. His grandson, Gavin Henderson, was of a different cloth. A pacifist and London County Councillor, he turned post-war Buscot into a Socialist salon, adding works by contemporary painters. The house was one of several bought after the Second World War for the National Trust by Ernest Cook and then leased back to the original owners. The present Lord Faringdon maintains the house and its collecting tradition today.

Buscot is reached from the Faringdon road through a stately copse of limes. The drive passes a lake, stables and formal gardens, stretched out like an apron in front of the house. These were designed by the Edwardian firm of Sir Ernest George & Peto. The house exterior is rectangular and of little interest, although Felix Kelly's depiction in the guidebook gives it a mystic charm. The architect was James Darley, the work much altered in the 20th century.

The appeal of Buscot lies in its pictures and their often idiosyncratic settings. The hall is an immediate surprise, like the entrance to a mansion in a Parisian boulevard. A suite of Regency neo-Egyptian furniture is overlooked by a della Robbia panel. Behind are two scagliola columns backed by *trompe-l'œil* trophies and French Empire furniture. Having begun thus, Buscot proceeds from surprise to delight.

Above After Lord Faringdon had bought Edward Burne-Jones' paintings of the *Legend of the Briar Rose* and brought them back to Buscot Park, he commissioned the artist to provide them with a suitable setting. Burne-Jones created a gilded carved frame that ran around the saloon and painted ten new panels to go between the main pictures. Essentially the story of Sleeping Beauty by another name, the Briar Rose legend was one of Burne-Jones' favourite subjects.

Buscot's character lies in its paintings not being inherited and left to hang where they 'always were' but in being bought to decorate a room. The room was then designed round them. The morning room is Dutch, with Rembrandt's *Pieter Six*, and other pictures by Rubens and van Dyck. Two tortoiseshell cabinets date from the same period. The dining room is bright red, inflaming landscapes by Wilson and Ibbetson and a picture composed of kingfisher feathers.

The saloon ceiling was reputedly by Adam's stuccoist, Joseph Rose, fit setting for Burne-Jones. Beyond is the 'Raphaelite' drawing room, bright yellow and hung with Italian Renaissance works, including Palma Vecchio and two tondos after Leonardo and Botticelli. Pictures follow fast and furious. Old Masters, drawings, sculptures peer down from the walls. A Rossetti of William Morris's wife, Janey, as Pandora gazes wistfully from a mantelpiece. A huge state bed looms behind a door. The sitting room is filled with pleasantly sentimental works by Reynolds.

The tradition of patronage continues in the garden, where frescos adorn summer-houses and swimming pools. A ferocious modern mural of the Faringdon family is in the tea-room.

Chastleton house

✪ ✪ ✪ ✩ Jacobean mansion with its contents and atmosphere intact

At Chastleton, 6 miles NE of Stow-on-the-Wold; National Trust, open part year by arrangement

Chastleton could be nowhere but in the heart of England, and dating from the heart of English history, the 17th century. When, in 1936, the estate farm had to be sold, the owner apologized to the staff, explaining that the family had 'lost all our money in the war'. She meant the Civil War. The house lies in a fold of the Cotswolds, its sandstone walls glowing with lichen and turning from crimson to ochre to grey depending on the light. Its builder in 1609 was a Welsh wool merchant turned lawyer, Walter Jones, with no great fortune or family connection. The Joneses were Royalist and remained Jacobite into the next century. It did them neither harm nor good. Nothing interesting happened here, except the invention of the rules of croquet (in 1868).

'... the house is a **quiet meander** through **time.**'

When I first visited Chastleton before its acquisition by the National Trust, its condition was as romantic as it was desperate. Damp dripped from walls. Dust lay thick beneath the cobwebs, birds occupied the attics and the garden was a jungle. Not until 1991 did Jones's descendants give up the ghost. Mrs Clutton-Brock, the last owner, excused the dust and cobwebs as 'accentuating the contours of the furniture'. She said the cobwebs should always be retained as 'they hold the place together'. Apart from the cobwebs, the Trust decided to 'conserve as found'. For once the policy did not seem pedantic. Nothing was altered, from the broken badminton racket inside the front door to the servants' bath in the rafters. Symbolic of revival, the topiary hedge, twice replanted, is being coaxed back to life. It is an astonishing creation. A galleon, a cat, a horse, a squirrel and other animals are just recognizable. In an autumn mist, these shapes rise and wander down the ages, like the house itself. A King Charles Oak and Jacobite Scots pine stand in the adjacent meadow, emblems of Jones's loyalty.

The exterior of Chastleton is old-fashioned. Jones wanted a symmetrical design with pedimented gables, yet in a style suggesting ancient occupation. The plan is still 16th-century, with stair towers at each side, tall mullioned windows and a Great Hall with screens passage. The entrance had to be

Above This detail of an owl can be found among the tapestries in Mrs Clutton-Brock's bedroom.

Below The Fettiplace Chamber is hung with Flemish tapestries that show the biblical story of Jacob. Woven around the turn of the 17th century they have hung at Chastleton House since at least 1633. When Henry Jones married into the influential Fettiplace family (see Kingston Bagpuize House, page 132) in 1609, the room was being built and his wife Anne's family arms were included in the decoration of the overmantel. **Right** The Long Gallery runs the length of the second floor. Its Jacobean barrel-vaulted ceiling, which spans the width of the room, is covered with intricate plasterwork.

tucked uncomfortably into the side of the projecting porch. This feature is shared with Smythson's Burton Agnes, in East Yorkshire. There may even have been a Smythson involvement at Chastleton.

The house interior honours Jones's desire to infuse his name with antiquity, architecture standing proxy for ancestry. The rooms are arranged on three floors round a central well. The hall is medieval in plan, its long oak table constructed *in situ*. Beyond are the formal reception rooms, the White Parlour and Great Parlour, both with rich plasterwork and chunky Jacobean friezes. The latter has a French tapestry depicting not the usual military or mythical scenes but a music party in a garden.

The east staircase with obelisk finials rises to the Great Chamber and the more important bedrooms. The grandest of these, the Fettiplace Room, was named after the Oxfordshire family into which Jones proudly married his son, Henry. The entire room is clothed, with carpets, curtains, bed covers and tapestries. The closet beyond has

'Here the family would have **promenaded** on **rainy days ...**'

flame-stitch fabric as old as the house. At the rear of this range is the Great Chamber, used to receive special guests or, in the 20th century, for giving Christmas presents to the estate staff. The topiary garden was designed to be seen from these windows.

The rest of the house is a quiet meander through time. Pictures, tapestries and furniture are not grand, the more precious for being of the period and continuously in the rooms. The Cavalier Room has a secret chamber. The Sheldon Room has a classical fireplace. The library has a rare King Charles Bible, believed to have been present with him on his scaffold and thus a precious heirloom.

The Long Gallery fills the rear of the second floor and is a superb example of the form. The barrel vault carries Jacobean scrollwork. Here the family would have promenaded on rainy days and enjoyed music and entertainment. The guidebook suggests that it is 'best in stormy conditions when the rain beats against the casements and the floor creaks underfoot like the deck of a ship in heavy seas'. Next door are the attics, including bleak servants' quarters buried among the family memorabilia.

The basements contain pantries, sculleries and kitchens, all left in some undefinably antique state. The Victorian range, with its pots and pans, was still in use in the 1950s. In the beer cellar is the celebrated Chastleton ladder, a battered giant once used to clear gutters at the highest point of the house. It would give modern health-and-safety officials a fit.

Cogges manor

★ Manorial farmhouse restored to the Victorian period

At Witney, 10 miles NW of Oxford; museum, open part year

Suburban Witney presses hard round the old manorial settlement at Cogges. The model farm is for children, the pigs and cows kept like creatures in a zoo. But the old manor survives, reflecting the changing fortunes of big houses near manufacturing towns. The building, still in part medieval, was a farmhouse, then home to a Witney woollen draper, boarding school and, finally at the turn of the 20th century, back to farm again. The museum decided to 'stop the clock' with this last use.

The interior is that of the Mawles family, the figures portrayed in straitened times at the end of the agricultural depression. The parlour is furnished with the familiar clutter of a Victorian drawing room. The dining room is panelled, with a sideboard decorated with Staffordshire pottery. Games are laid out on the table, ready to be played.

Cogges has well-furnished kitchens and pantries, with a lit fire in the former. Upstairs the bedrooms are shabbily genteel. There is one oddity, a panelled 17th-century study in which a waxwork Mr Blake, the Witney draper, is lost in thought. Surely he must be wondering at his anachronistic survival in a house dedicated to Victoriana.

Ditchley park

★★★ House by James Gibbs with interiors by William Kent

At Enstone, 13 miles NW of Oxford; private house, open by arrangement

Ditchley is a magnificent if rather bloodless mansion. It is now a conference centre dedicated to the cause of Anglo-American relations and is kept as immaculate as that implies. The house was built in 1720–6 for George Lee, 2nd Earl of Lichfield, whose father at the age of eleven had married Charlotte Fitzroy, illegitimate daughter of Charles II by Barbara Villiers. The architect was Francis Smith of Warwick, his design modified by James Gibbs. Also involved were William Kent and Henry Flitcroft.

Ditchley was sold by the Lee-Dillon family in 1933 to an anglicized American couple, Ronald and Nancy Tree, who were already tenants of Gibbs's Kelmarsh Hall in Northamptonshire. They were lavish entertainers and offered the house to Churchill for occasional weekends during the Second World War when Chequers was considered unsafe. In 1947 Nancy and Ronald parted, she to marry the owner of Kelmarsh. In 1953, the house was bought by the Wills family who established the present trust.

The exterior of Ditchley is the epitome of early Georgian restraint. Gibbs wrote that grace and beauty in a building lie not in 'the Bulk of Fabrick, the Richness and Quality of the Materials, the Multiplicity of Lines, nor the Gaudiness of the Finishing ... but in the Proportion of the Parts to one another and to the whole'.

The entrance façade is a seemly rectangle, balanced by flanking pavilions reached by quadrant colonnades. The only sign of frivolity on the exterior are the lead figures that adorn the roof. They look as if lost on their way to Blenheim.

The interior is wholly different in temperament, a riot of plasterwork and ornament. Ditchley is exceptional among early Georgian houses in its lack of Victorian alteration. The hall of 1724–5 is supremely lovely, a masterpiece by William Kent and not overstated. The marble floor offsets the chimneypiece and the majestic doorcase to the saloon. Both support reclining figures of the arts and sciences. At modern-day Ditchley, such figures would need to depict politics, economics and international relations.

Above When Ronald and Nancy Tree bought Ditchley Park in 1933, the house was unmodernized, with no heating system and only one bathroom. The saloon was where the former owner, Lord Dillon, reputedly took his baths, in front of the fireplace. The Trees transformed Ditchley into a much more comfortable home and played host to many important guests; when Churchill stayed during the war, he held several secret meetings here with members of the American government.

Ditchley's hall is complemented by its saloon, one of the finest such 'double acts' in early Georgian design. While the hall has the relative simplicity of an atrium, its walls imitating an exterior, the saloon is all interior. Ionic pilasters uphold a deep frieze and rich ceiling. The craftsmen were Vassalli and the Artari brothers.

In the saloon overmantels of the doors and niches are of Baroque fecundity and a complete contrast with the sedate hall. Antlers are mounted on the wall, reputedly surviving from an earlier Lee house on the site and recalling its early use as a hunting lodge. They seem a deliberate anachronism, as if determined to mock the Artaris' subtle harmonies, like bagpipes intruding on a minuet. Large windows offer a vista of sky and meadows falling away to a lake surrounded by temples in the distance.

The entire ground floor at Ditchley is composed of reception rooms, their decoration rich and most distracting to bored conferees. The Velvet Room was once the state bedroom, with a painting of Rome by Panini and Indian satin wall-hangings. The White Drawing Room is a controlled burst of gilded plasterwork on white background, almost as exuberant as the saloon. The pictures are by Lely and Kneller of the Earl's grandparents, Charles II and the Duchess of Cleveland. In keeping with the modernity of the theme, Ditchley might perhaps dip a toe into more contemporary works of art.

Ewelme almshouses

When southern England is all suburb, there will still be Ewelme. It is hidden in a fold on the edge of the Chilterns, surrounded by hills and fields, a beautiful grouping of big house, farm, school and church. At its heart is a quadrangle of redbrick almshouses.

They were built by William de la Pole, Duke of Suffolk, and his wife Alice Chaucer, granddaughter of the poet. The year was 1437 in the troubled reign of Henry VI. Ewelme school was founded at the same time as the king was founding its more famous contemporary at Eton. It now claims to be the oldest church school in the country. The buildings were of brick, in a chalk landscape where timber and daub were the usual material. The masons probably came from Suffolk's East Anglian estates.

The almshouses lie down a covered way from the west door of the church. The doors are panelled and guarded by angels with extravagant head-dresses. The thirteen cottages flank a quadrangle, no longer thatched but with tiled roofs swooping over the cloistered walks. Gabled dormers on each side have pretty bargeboards. The cobbled quadrangle contains a well and, with its colourful potted flowers, is most picturesque.

The almshouses are still occupied by almsmen who say daily prayers for their founders' souls, in accordance with the statutes. The Master's House is occupied by the head of the local primary school, again, as always. This is a village welfare state as it should – and could – be across much of rural England.

Greys court

I cannot rid my mind of Greys Court being once occupied by William Knollys, said to be origin of Shakespeare's Malvolio. Was it in this hall that he received his fake letter of love? Was it in this ancient tower that he was humiliated? The big house has mostly gone and Malvolio's ghost, if here it be, must be wandering this lovely Chiltern combe a sad-faced vagrant.

The true heroes of Greys Court were quite different. They were the Brunners. Sir John Brunner and his business partner, Ludwig Mond, were Victorian immigrants who together founded ICI at Winnington, in Cheshire, in the 1870s. In 1937, Sir John's grandson, Sir Felix Brunner, acquired the remains of Elizabethan Greys outside Henley and set to work on their rescue. These comprised a picturesque set of brick and flint buildings round the old courtyard, including a 14th-century tower at one corner and two octagonal Tudor ones at another.

The present house is a fragment of a wing of the old mansion. It has a triple-gabled façade and is built in a warm mixture of brick and flint. A side entrance is overlooked by a pretty brick oriel window of *c*1570, next to a wall carrying four statues of naked cherubs with helmets.

On the other side is an 18th-century extension, a modestly grand work with a bow window in rusticated stone. The architect was possibly Henry Keene.

The house interior is simple, with one exception. The entrance hall is stone-floored with niches filled with porcelain. A square table is Swiss, from the Brunners' homeland, dated 1584 and with a German inscription recording its commissioning by an earlier Felix Brunner. Behind are the 16th-century kitchens.

The most spectacular room is the 18th-century drawing room to the right of the hall. The walls and ceiling are superbly decorated by Roberts of Oxford, whose robust English Rococo can also be seen at Rousham (see page 142). Similar plasterwork adorns the old dining room, later converted as a family schoolroom.

The charming outbuildings include a donkey wheel for drawing water from the old well. It was in use until 1914. Greys has grounds covering the surrounding slopes, punctuated by pines and beeches that gloriously clothe these flanks of the Chilterns.

Kelmscott manor

Right The tapestry room is hung with four 17th-century Flemish tapestries, part of a series at Kelmscott that depicts the life of Samson. They were left in the house by the Turner family, who leased the manor to William Morris in 1871, and are believed to have been at Kelmscott since the early 18th century. Morris described them as a 'pleasant background for the living people who haunt the room'.

★★★ Tudor farmhouse and country retreat of William Morris and his family

At Kelmscott, 9 miles SW of Witney; private house, open part year

In 1871, William Morris's beautiful wife, Janey, was embroiled in a love affair with his friend, Dante Gabriel Rossetti. The tolerant Morris decided to move her with their two daughters and Rossetti away from the noise, dirt and scandal of London. He found them a secluded farmhouse in Oxfordshire. 'Please, dear Janey, be happy,' he said and vanished on a walking tour of Iceland.

The house was as inconspicuous as could be imagined, in a hamlet by the 'stripling Thames'. The manor stood next to a farm and a garden stretched down to the river. The Cotswold stone was grey-green. The buildings, said Janey, were in a 'purring state of comfort ... if you were to stroke them they would move'. Here Janey and Rossetti were briefly happy. Morris was not. In November 1872, he wrote to a friend, Aglaia Coronio, that 'Rossetti has set himself down at Kelmscott as if he never meant to go away ... he has all sorts of ways so unsympathetic with the sweet simple old place that I feel his presence a kind of slur.'

Rossetti's mental collapse and departure three years later meant that Morris was able to repossess Kelmscott until he died. It was his country idyll. Its antiquity, seclusion and introversion fitted his anti-industrial idealism. Here it was safe to be socialist and easy to be medieval. At Kelmscott, one can sense Morris's romance with nature and with the texture of man-made things. He used it as the frontispiece of his utopian novel, *News from Nowhere, an Epoch of Rest*.

Morris's daughter, May, lived at Kelmscott with her friend, Frances Lobb, until her death in 1938, leaving it as memorial to her father. Many of the furnishings were brought from Morris's London home at Hammersmith. The house is a 16th-century farm, with parlour rather than Great Hall, a screens passage and two extended wings. One of these was added in 1670 with big gables and tiny pediments over the attic windows. The interior is Morrisonian Tudor. Every inch is hung with Morris fabrics and paper. Yet the dominant personality is Janey. Pictures of her by Rossetti and Burne-Jones seem to start from every wall, her beauty retained even in old age. Her needlework is very evident. On a corner of an embroidered counterpane she depicted Kelmscott, as in an act of private homage.

The parlour has a wide fireplace and simple country furniture. The chintz hangings are Morris's popular 'Strawberry thief': the theme of a thrush taking a strawberry was said to have been witnessed by Morris in the Kelmscott garden. Beyond is the garden hall with a large unfinished embroidery

Below The bed in William Morris's room is an early 17th-century oak four-poster and is hung with a valance embroidered by his daughter May with the poem 'For the Bed at Kelmscott', written by Morris in 1891. The bedspread, embroidered by Janey in around 1895, includes a quote from another Morris poem, 'A Garden by the Sea'.

Above Beneath the roofs of Kelmscott are a series of attic rooms, described by Morris in *News from Nowhere* (1890) as 'quaint garrets amongst the great timbers'. Today the rooms are filled with textiles and furnishings designed by Morris or by his friends and professional partners, such as Edward Burne-Jones, Philip Webb and Ford Maddox Brown.

showing Janey as Queen Guinevere, a Pre-Raphaelite icon. Another tapestry was woven entirely by Morris in 1879, suggesting extraordinary industry for such a busy man. The room contains a settle designed by Philip Webb with a decorated hood.

The panelled room beyond is 17th century, with pilasters and a rustic Brueghel above the fireplace. Here hangs Rossetti's exquisite portrait of Janey in a blue silk dress. The Green Room displays Morris's own first embroidery of 1857. It is in rough simple stitches, with his enigmatic motto borrowed from van Eyck, 'If I can'.

Upstairs is Mrs Morris's Bedroom hung with Willow Bough wallpaper. Across the landing is Morris's bedroom. The bed is hung with a pelmet embroidered by May Morris with a poem in medieval script, the coverlet embroidered by Janey. It is a room full of colour and peace.

When Morris took the house it contained tapestries depicting the story of Samson. Morris loved their faded state, their brightness lost and 'nothing left but the indigo blues, the greys and warm yellow browns'. It gave 'an air of romance that nothing else would quite do'. In the tapestry room is a photograph of Janey, still beautiful at seventy.

The house needs more of Morris's 'fadedness'. In the attics he had loved 'the great timbers of the roof, where of old time the tillers and herdsmen of the manor slept'. In his day they were still filled with 'the litter of useless and disregarded matters – bunches of dying flowers, feathers of birds, shells of starlings' eggs, caddis worms in mugs, and the like'. The attics are now filled with pristine fabric displays.

Kingston Bagpuize house

⭐⭐ An early Georgian house with Rococo staircase

At Kingston Bagpuize, 9 miles SW of Oxford; private house, open part year

The house belonged to the ubiquitous Thames valley grandees, the Fettiplaces, into whose family Walter Jones of Chastleton (see page 122) was so eager for his son to marry. Edmund Fettiplace acquired it in the 1670s and his descendants remained here until 1917. Since then Kingston Bagpuize has passed through many hands and is now owned and well maintained by Mrs Grant. The house was rebuilt in the 1720s, probably by one of the Townesend family of builders from Oxford.

Seen from the main road, the house has a guard of honour of beeches, commanded by two giant Wellingtonias. The style is early Georgian, front and back almost identical, as are the two sides. The exterior is mildly Baroque, each elevation pedimented and with decorative urns. The walls are of redbrick with stone quoins and elegant surrounds to the windows and doors.

The old entrance hall in the middle of the main façade is now the drawing room. As often with Georgian buildings, the house was later 'reversed'. Entry is now from a new drive at the back. The door is placed uncomfortably beneath the main staircase.

This staircase is Kingston Bagpuize's best feature. It is of pine and oak rising in lighthearted skips past swirling wainscoting to a shell-capped niche on the landing. The walls are hung with hand-painted Chinese paper, installed in the 1950s and not quite fitting. The whole composition is Rococo and fun. The library is charmingly hung with pictures of the children of the house over the years. A smaller sitting room has curious floating pediments over the doors, a 20th-century conceit.

Mapledurham house

★★★ An Elizabethan mansion set in a medieval enclave on the Thames

At Mapledurham, 4 miles NW of Reading; private house, open part year

Alexander Pope, the poet, was a lifelong friend of two daughters of Mapledurham, Teresa and Martha Blount. When Martha fell ill with smallpox and could not go to George I's coronation, her elder sister went alone. Pope's poem 'To Miss Blount, on her leaving the Town, after the Coronation' teased Teresa on the contrast between her experiences in London and her return to Mapledurham and to 'plain-work, and to purling brooks,/Old-fashion'd halls, dull aunts and croaking rooks.' Pope well describes this ancient mansion on the banks of the Thames opposite Reading.

The best view of Mapledurham is from the approach past the church. A relic of the original manor fills the foreground while the chimneys and dormers of the great house rise behind. The Middle Ages are thus seen against a Jacobean backdrop, the latter of 1608–12. The Blount family have lived on this spot since 1490. It is still occupied by their descendants, now Eystons.

The house and its settlement are as rural now as it would have been when, in 1828, Michael Blount decided on drastic modernization. He stripped out most of the ancient interior yet restored the ancient exterior. He kept the old stables, church and almshouses lining the road and left the house

Above The Great Parlour at Mapledurham is furnished with a comfortable mix of fine antiques and well-worn family furniture. Portraits of past Blounts look down from the walls. The family, who claim Norman descent, have owned Mapledurham since 1490 when Richard Blount of Iver bought the manor.

itself ostensibly early 17th century. Like many formerly recusant Catholics, he found in old architecture the comfort of the old religion.

The house is H-plan, its wings flanking a shallow courtyard, with porch and symmetrical façade. By the 1600s, Great Halls had already shrunk to entrance halls, with reception rooms above. In this hall, a sinister Dobson portrait of the Royalist, Sir Charles Blount, hangs over the mantelpiece. On the walls are carved animal heads, including a 'wolf in sheep's clothing'. The adjacent library has a collection of recusant books and numerous Blount portraits.

To the rear of the hall is the family chapel, built after the Catholic Emancipation Act of 1791. The interior is Gothick, like that at Milton (see right), the passage outside lined with drawings of Sir Thomas More and his family. The staircase to the first floor is Jacobean, of dark oak, cantilevered and not supported on newel posts. The Great Parlour upstairs runs the width of the house, its former rear windows blocked off. It has a fine strapwork ceiling, with Blount portraits on pale green walls and views over the park from the remaining windows. The dining room downstairs contains an exquisite painting by William Larkin of *Lady St John of Bletso*, *c*1615. Its detailed sylvan background is said to qualify it as one of the earliest English landscapes.

Milton Manor house

★ ☆ Restoration mansion with a Gothick library

At Milton, 9 miles S of Oxford; private house, open part year

Few houses cling more desperately to their dignity than Milton. This faded Restoration mansion hangs on to life between the roaring A34 and the sprawl of Didcot, its grounds unkempt and cement filling the gaps in its pilasters and quoins. The house was built sometime after 1663, Dutch and wayward. It was sold to the Barrett family, City lacemakers and devout Catholics who, in 1764, added wings with Gothick interiors. The Mockler-Barrett family own it to this day, one of that band of saints who uphold great houses in defiance of financial gravity.

The façades to back and front are monumentally grand beneath a pitched roof with deep overhanging eaves. The entrance front has thin pilasters with Ionic capitals rising the full height of the wall. They are adorned with unusual garters of fleur-de-lys 'jewels' and have been crudely restored. They need attention when money can be found.

Of the downstairs rooms, the hall fireplace is a florid 17th-century work with rustic maidens lolling above a painting of exotic birds. Milton's masterpiece is its Gothick library, designed in the

'The façades to back and front are monumentally grand...'

1760s by Stephen Wright. Windows and bookcases are crowned with ogival decoration, encrusted with crockets and trefoils. Display cases also contain teapots collected by successive Mocklers. A set of Pinxton china was made especially for Milton in the 1790s, with a picture of the house on every piece. A cup and a saucer went to the 'Treasure Houses of Britain' exhibition in Washington in 1985.

The house interior is dominated by a 17th-century oak staircase from ground floor to attic. Its handrails have chunky balusters and massive newel posts. Yet at each landing the 18th century takes over, with delicate arches to the passages. One leads to the Barretts' private Roman Catholic chapel. The ceiling has pendants and the walls are decorated with blind arcading and ogee window arches. The 'wedding cake' effect is similar to that of Shobdon church in Herefordshire. Valuable medieval and 16th-century glass has been imported for the windows. The chapel is still in use. The chinoiserie bedroom next door has beautiful hand-painted wallpaper and marquetry furniture.

Above Ogee arches top the bookcases and windows of the Gothick library at Milton Manor; they were carved by Richard Lawrence, a master craftsman from London. Today, some of the bookcases hold displays of the Mockler family's collection of late 18th- and 19th-century English porcelain. The room was created by Bryant Barrett, lacemaker to George III, and his architect Stephen Wright; a group portrait of Barrett and his family by Joseph Highmore hangs over the fireplace.

Minster Lovell hall

⭐ Riverside remains of a once-great 15th-century house

At Minster Lovell, 3 mile W of Witney; English Heritage, open all year

Minster Lovell was home to one of England's great families, the Lovells, who lived adjacent to the old monastery from the 12th century. The present building was erected in the 1430s when the Lovells were a power in the land, but they never recovered from their loyalty to Richard III at Bosworth. The house passed to the Crown and was bought by the Cokes of Holkham in Norfolk in 1602. They dismantled much of the old house in the 18th century. Its ruins stand amid trees on the banks of the River Windrush, with the minster church, manor and dovecote close by. The outline of the original courtyard can clearly be seen in the grass.

A cobbled pathway leads across what would have been an outer court to the main gate and Great Hall. The porch has a complex ribbed vault inside. The hall itself is astonishingly high, lit by two lofty windows on one side and smaller ones on top of the chapel on the other. Traces of wall plaster survive. This must have been an awesome chamber. Beyond it is the solar, still with its fireplace, and a Great Chamber with traceried windows. Also surviving is a south-west tower by the river, with an impressive chimney and fragments of a spiral staircase. This was built after the main house, presumably for private apartments.

The joy of Minster Lovell is the serenity of its setting. It is easy in such places for the mind's eye to bring a ruin back to life.

Nuffield place

⭐ Thirties-style home of motoring entrepreneur and philanthropist

At Nuffield, 7 miles NW of Henley-on-Thames; private house, currently closed

Nuffield was for thirty years home to the richest man in England, William Morris. He was founder of Morris Motors in Oxford, and later became Lord Nuffield. Built in 1914, the house was bought in 1933 and extended by Morris and his wife. It survives as a fully furnished work of the mid-twentieth century and a memorial to a most unostentatious tycoon and philanthropist.

Morris was born in 1877 and left school at fifteen. A youthful cycling champion, he set up a bicycle repair business in Oxford with £4 of capital. He went on to build motorbikes and then cars, making 400 Morris cars at his Cowley works in 1919. Six years later his annual output was 56,000. With no children, he gave away all the money he made, mostly to medicine and education. The Nuffield Foundation was and still is one of the wealthiest charities in England. The house is held in trust by Nuffield College, Oxford.

The architect was Oswald Milne, a pupil of Lutyens and designed in his master's 'Queen Anne' style. Nuffield was conservative, indeed Edwardian, in taste. The rooms might be those of any comfortable suburban villa, the furniture mostly reproduction pieces from the Oxford firm of Cecil Halliday.

The general effect can seem charmless but the interior is uplifted by mementoes of Nuffield's various interests, notably his love of gadgets, and his lifelong passion for smoking and golf. The house is exactly as he left it, apart from an apparent lightening of the paint schemes.

The hall is filled with long-case clocks, which Nuffield tended and repaired himself. In the drawing room are Lalique lamps, a radiogram and an ingenious 'self-lighting match dispenser'. The sitting room contains an HMV television, costing £110 in 1955. Everywhere are models of cars. The upstairs bedrooms are simple for so rich a man. Lalique appears as the one extravagance. Lady Nuffield's bed is turned at an angle to give her a view of the garden.

Lord Nuffield's bedroom is the star of the house. It is starkly plain, as if harking back to his simple boyhood in the backstreets of Oxford. The carpet is said to be patched from the floorings of his cars and certainly looks it. A suite of cupboards is devoted not to clothes but to a miniature workshop, crammed with do-it-yourself tools, which he used when he could not sleep. Nuffield even mended his own shoes. He took a tool kit with him wherever he went, including on sea voyages. His Heath-Robinson lighting system survives over the bed.

So simple are these rooms that the Coronation robes on display in the dressing room come as a shock. Would Nuffield have permitted this kind of ostentation?

Downstairs is his exercise horse and an iron lung, a machine of which he was an early sponsor. He also sponsored Borstal institutions for young offenders but was appalled when the Home Office opened one next door to his house. Lady Nuffield never quite recovered from the shock.

'The interior is **uplifted** by mementoes of **Nuffield's various interests** ...'

Nuneham Courtenay

★★ Palladian villa, now much altered, within Capability Brown grounds

Near Nuneham Courtenay, 5 miles S of Oxford; private house, open by arrangement

Have you come for enlightenment, I was asked at Nuneham. I had indeed, although not the enlightenment offered by the 'global retreat of the Brahma Kumaris World Spiritual University'. The walls are festooned with mandalas and diagrams of the Path to Knowledge. Carpets are deep and rooms are set aside for meditation. Eager students in tennis shoes and white-garmented teachers float silently through the building. The mansion of the Harcourts has, since the Second World War, been a college of education and a Rothmans International conference centre. Its new incarnation came as a shock, but the house is in good, and welcoming, hands.

The site was chosen in 1755 by the 1st Earl Harcourt of Stanton Harcourt as the spot for his new Palladian villa in an Arcadian landscape. The old riverside village was demolished and a new one built along the Oxford road, a mile to the east. This apparent outrage gave rise to Goldsmith's celebrated poem, 'The Deserted Village', deploring the removal of ancient settlements for aristocratic pleasure parks. 'Thus fares the land by luxury betrayed ... The country blooms – a garden and a grave'.

The ground for the house ran down to the Thames, with the spires of Oxford visible in the distance. The architect was Stiff Leadbetter and a shortage of stone meant the old house at Stanton Harcourt had to be demolished and its blocks floated down the Thames on barges. Nuneham was not intended as a great mansion. It embodied the new mid-Georgian fashion for the villa as the suitable form for a nobleman's country seat.

Nemesis for the removal of the village was at hand. The 1st Earl had not been long in his new home when, in 1777, he died when rescuing his dog from a well. His son was a rebellious follower of Rousseau, and remarked that he could wish only his worst enemy 'a title, a large acquaintance and a place in the country'. They were, he said, incitements to flattery and cheating. The young man disposed of all royal portraits in the house and prepared the tenantry for republican citizenship. Yet he was soon converted by the favour of George III and he and his wife became courtiers. Capability

Below The staircase at Nuneham is by Capability Brown, who was brought in to work on the house and park in 1778. Probably England's most famous landscape gardener, Brown's work as an architect is often overlooked and he designed several Palladian country villas, beginning with Croome Court (Worcestershire) in 1751.

Brown arrived, the house was extended and the grounds 'improved'. Work continued with Henry Holland and later Sir Robert Smirke.

Despite heavy wings and extensions, Nuneham is still at heart a quiet Palladian villa. Especially dignified is the garden façade, with canted central bay and Venetian windows to take advantage of the view. Of the much-altered interiors, Capability Brown's staircase with iron balusters survives, rising to an oval skylight.

On the first floor, the Octagon Room has Rococo plasterwork and a magnificent floral roundel installed by Holland. The drawing room and dining room retain their fireplaces, ceilings and Venetian window. The gilding in the former goes well with the Hindu decor. The dining room chimneypiece is by Athenian Stuart.

Horace Walpole thought the grounds at Nuneham the most beautiful in England. They are still well tended but lack their original panache and the vista to Oxford.

Rousham park

★★★ Jacobean house set in grounds landscaped by William Kent

At Rousham, 12 miles N of Oxford; private house, open by arrangement, gardens open all year

Rousham was meant to be a rural Chiswick House. But here there is no National Trust or English Heritage to discipline nature. The Augustan vista is mildly overgrown and the genius of the place has aged with dignity. The landscape is the work of William Kent. It still shows the Eyecatcher ruin, the Temple, the Venus Vale, the arched Praeneste, the Cascade and even the long-horned cattle. Everything suggests antiquity.

Rousham was built *c*1635 for the Dormer family, whose descendants still occupy it. The Dormers were staunch Royalists, 'as we still are,' says the lady of the house. The manor suffered in the Civil War but the family fortunes recovered sufficiently for General Dormer in 1738 to commission William Kent to remodel the house and grounds. Horace Walpole called the result 'Kentissimo'.

The exterior is now 18th-century Gothic revival, retaining the Jacobean E-plan but marred by plate glass windows. The best feature of the entrance hall is its front door, surviving from the old house and with musket holes through which guns could be trained on attackers. The walls are lined with Dormer portraits by Lely, Johnson, Kneller and others.

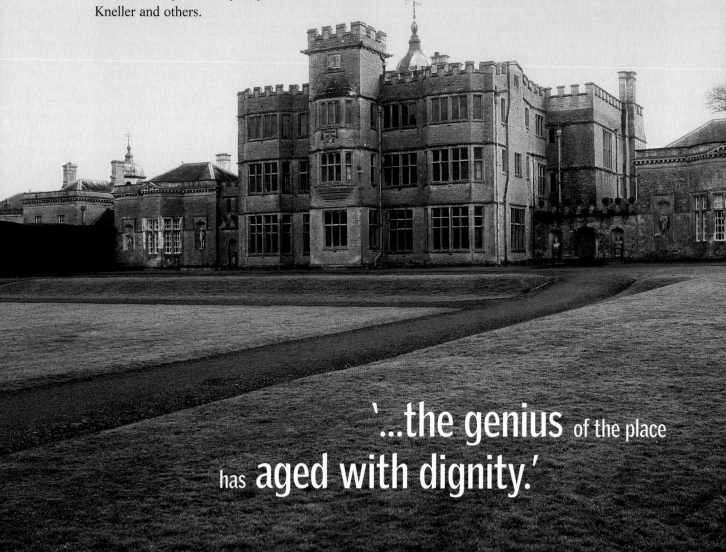

'...the genius of the place has aged with dignity.'

Above and right William Kent claimed that 'all gardening is landscape painting'. At Rousham Park, and at other gardens, he added features, such as the Temple of Echo and the statue of Pan, to draw the eye into the landscape, much as an artist would to create a focal point in a picture.

The finest room at Rousham is Kent's eccentric Painted Parlour, fashioned from the former kitchens. It is as handsome as anything at Chiswick, but in miniature and thus habitable. The decoration is a *tour de force* of classical motifs. Vitruvian curves and scrolls tumble over every surface in wavelets. Brackets support bronze statues. The overmantel rises past griffins to erupt in a broken pediment. Overhead is Kent's ceiling, painted on canvas in a pattern that looks forward to the Diocletan designs of Robert Adam. The panelling has been painted olive green.

The Great Parlour is also by Kent but re-fashioned in 1764 by Thomas Roberts of Oxford, an admirable provincial stuccoist who also worked at Greys Court. To him we owe the Rococo picture frames, dripping with plaster swags and Ho-Ho birds. The room contains an outstanding full-length portrait of Elizabeth I. A range of rooms along the garden front was added in the 1860s. Its dining room contains pictures of Civil War Dormers and the music room has much family paraphernalia, including a model of an old galleon.

Shipton-under-Wychwood:
Shaven Crown

★ Monastic guest house with surviving Great Hall

High Street, Shipton-under-Wychwood; now a hotel

The name refers to the monks who built the old house for visitors in the 15th century. It became an Elizabethan hunting lodge, as did many former monastic hostels, before reverting to do service as an inn, now a small hotel. The only reference to hunting in its current promotional literature is to 'antique-hunting'.

The main entrance arch has a square hood. The original hall survives to the left, with two strong gabled wings on either side projecting towards the road. They have stone-mullioned windows. The hall doubles as sitting room and hotel reception area and is still open to the roof, with complex wind-braces. Its window has Perpendicular tracery. Later stairs rise to what appears to be a minstrels' gallery with a fine battered fascia. The old parlour is now the restaurant.

The original courtyard survives to the rear, the ranges dating from the 16th and 17th centuries. The bar has a fire blazing in its ancient grate, as it must have done to welcome travellers for 500 years. The hotel entrance is marred by two gratuitous glass doors which should be removed.

Stonor

★★★ Medieval home with Georgian façade and Gothick additions

Near Stonor, 4 miles N of Henley-on-Thames; private house, open part year

Stonor lies in a fold of the Chilterns, utterly on its own. The Stonors, Lords Camoys, were and are resolute Roman Catholics and the house might be a monastery of ascetics concealed from the world. On its walls hang pictures of saints and bishops where would normally be ancestors. The library has one of the finest collections of recusant literature in England.

Stonors have lived on this spot for eight and a half centuries, defying Reformation and revolution. Mass has always been celebrated in this place. Not until 1975 did catastrophe threaten. The 6th Lord Camoys was so enraged by Labour's capital taxation that he sold the house and its contents and departed. Like the Bedingfelds of Oxburgh Hall in Norfolk, the family decided to buy it back. His son, the present Lord Camoys, then commenced a long campaign of restoration and refurnishing, assisted by other Stonors sending or lending family heirlooms. The rescue has been a total success.

The house is not grand. It is spread along the contour of the valley, with flanking ranges containing a 13th-century hall and solar. A new hall was added in the 14th century, producing an E-plan with Tudor forecourt two centuries later. Since the family were impoverished throughout the recusancy period, no rebuilding took place. Everything was adapted and squeezed to fit the narrow valley site, with the Chiltern hillside piling up behind. In the 18th century, the house received a redbrick Georgian façade and Gothick frontispiece with Elizabethan statues.

Almost all Stonor's interiors are newly decorated and furnished with works acquired, or re-acquired, by the present generation. Each room thus has a character of its own, designed by Lady Camoys in vivid colours. The principal rooms are along the main façade. The dining room is hung with French wallpaper of *c*1815, depicting Paris from the Seine. Lord Camoys' adjacent study has

Above The main hall at Stonor is part of the medieval core of the house and dates back to the 1350s. Much of the decoration, however, was added during the gothicization of Stonor in 1757. The room was reduced to its current size when it was divided up in 1834; the fireplace was moved to its present position at the same time.

Old Master drawings by Tiepolo and Carracci, and Venetian globes of 1699. The staircase to the bedroom floor is lined with a collection of silhouettes.

The first of the bedrooms has one of the most extraordinary beds I have seen. It is in the form of a shell floating on a sea of dolphins, surrounded by chairs shaped like oysters. The Walrus and the Carpenter seem about to dine. The library commemorates recusancy down the ages. It is filled with ancient missals, prayer books and Bibles, its ledges peopled not with classical worthies but with Baroque saints. A small exhibition celebrates St Edmund Campion who took refuge here during the Reformation. The Long Gallery to the rear contains three fine tapestries, one of them 17th-century Flemish, and a collection of modern ceramics from the Far East.

The family chapel is mostly a 1796 refit in the fashionable Gothick also employed in the chapels at Mapledurham (page 133) and Milton (page 135). It was repainted in mauve and pink by Osbert Lancaster and John Piper, with ogival doors and Catholic sculpture donated by Graham Greene.

Weston manor

⭐ Medieval manor house within a garden of yew topiary

At Weston-on-the-Green, 7 miles N of Oxford; now a hotel

The 16th-century manor belonged to the Norreys, Earls of Berkshire, then the Berties, Earls of Abingdon, who held it until 1917. It then passed through the Greville family, enduring many tribulations before becoming a luxury hotel in 1983.

Weston was lucky to have a 'good' 19th-century, when the stone façade was restored in neo-Jacobean style. Its entrance hall was given a ceiling with vigorous bosses in the 1920s. Behind is the old Tudor courtyard. This has been left crumbling and atmospheric and houses, most oddly, a set of Jacobean doors from Exeter College Chapel, Oxford. The original Great Hall is on the left, an important survival imported from Notley Abbey in Buckinghamshire. There would have been a further courtyard to the rear, one arm of which survives as an impossibly narrow range of bedrooms.

The hall interior is a mass of linenfold panelling rising past a carved frieze to a high open roof. The panelling also came from Notley Abbey in the 18th century. At one end is a deep minstrels' gallery. Almost all the rooms have Jacobean fireplaces, panelling and other features imported at some stage or other. The garden has a celebrated exhibition of topiary, with hedges and trees of all heights and shapes.

Oxford Colleges

All Souls college

✦✦ Medieval college with distinctive 18th-century towers by Hawksmoor

High Street, Oxford; private house, open all year

All Souls was founded in 1438 by the Archbishop of Canterbury, Henry Chichele, to educate priests and lawyers and to pray for the souls of all who fell in the French wars. It is exclusively for 'fellows' engaged in their own research or in public life, and has no undergraduates. Its buildings of 1441 along the High are equally unchanged, unexciting but medieval.

The entrance gatehouse faces the chapel on the far side of the quad. Although heavily restored by Sir Gilbert Scott, the great stone reredos survives, only the carved statues in the niches replacing those smashed by Reformation iconoclasts.

The style of the college now transforms itself from 15th to 18th century. The North Quad at All Souls was debated by the fellows, in true Oxford style, for the best part of a century. The burning question of Gothic or classical was never resolved until Hawksmoor took the bull by the horns. The result, commenced in 1715, is Oxford's most picturesque setting. The quad was described by critics as for lay fellows 'of great fortune and high birth, and of little morals and less learning'. Plans presented by Hawksmoor were extended when Christopher Codrington, a sugar planter and bibliophile, left money for a new library.

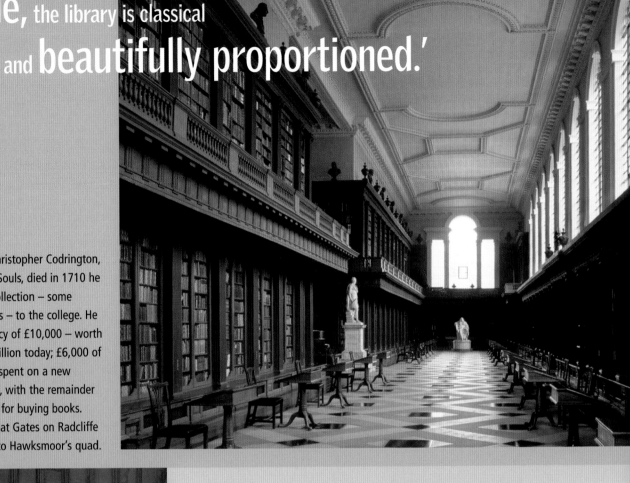

'... inside, the library is classical and beautifully proportioned.'

Right When Christopher Codrington, a fellow of All Souls, died in 1710 he left his book collection – some 12,000 volumes – to the college. He also left a legacy of £10,000 – worth more than a million today; £6,000 of this was to be spent on a new library building, with the remainder to be set aside for buying books. **Below** The Great Gates on Radcliffe Square look into Hawksmoor's quad.

Hawksmoor's design was 'in the Gothick manner' out of respect for the front quad and with the admirable explanation that 'whatever is good in its kinde ought to be preserv'd in respect to antiquity ... for destruction can be profitable to none but Such as Live by it'. The result is a three-sided court facing Radcliffe Square through a screen. This has a Gothic folly as its centrepiece, crowned with a Corinthian capital and a pineapple urn, a delightful architectural joke. Hawksmoor felt his quad needed some more assertive signature and thus balanced the screen with two Gothic towers with telescopic lanterns on top. Again, they are follies, carrying neither bells within nor rooms beneath. They are now integral to the Oxford skyline, a Gothic counterpoint to James Gibbs's classical Radcliffe Camera, as the Gibbs Building in Cambridge answers to King's College Chapel.

The other two sides of the new quad were also intended to balance. The exterior of the Codrington Library of 1716 was designed to respond to the Gothic of the old chapel facing it. Yet inside, the library is classical and beautifully proportioned. Hawksmoor's chief problem was with the end window, which had to be Palladian within and Gothic without.

Balliol college

Balliol claims to be the oldest scholarly community in Oxford, founded as a penance demanded of a 13th-century northerner, John de Balliol, for kidnapping a bishop. He was ordered to support 'sixteen poor scholars' at the then fledgling university at Oxford. British penal policy has gone downhill ever since. Balliol's widow, named Dervorguilla, founded the college in 1282, outside the city wall and beyond what is now the Broad.

The present buildings are of interest for their 19th-century rebuilding by two masters of the Gothic revival, William Butterfield and Alfred Waterhouse. They were commissioned by Balliol's celebrated Victorian Masters, Richard Jenkyns and Benjamin Jowett. Of Jowett, it was said (by him) that 'what I don't know isn't knowledge'. The Front Quad entrance and façade are by Waterhouse, in a tedious Gothic revival style. Waterhouse was said to have based his entrance on a design by A. W. N. Pugin, rejected as excessively zealous. Pugin had intended the rooms to have prayer alcoves with religious texts on the walls. In the road opposite, Cranmer, Latymer and Ridley were burned at the stake during the Marian Counter-Reformation.

(In my day a then down-market Randolph Hotel was offering steaks 'cooked Cranmer, Latymer or Ridley?')

Inside, Waterhouse's entrance clashes with Butterfield's chapel across the Front Quad. The chapel has Butterfield's characteristic polychrome-banded stonework. The building was so hated by the Edwardians that it was almost demolished in 1912. Next to it lies what remains of the medieval college, the old library of 1431.

The Garden Quad beyond is formed of a series of mostly Victorian buildings backing onto St Giles. In the middle is Waterhouse's hall, more successful than his Front Quad building. The style is medieval, with bold buttresses and steep-pitched roof. Its stern gothicism was long the butt of high-living Trinity undergraduates next door, who would regularly festoon the roof with paint, obscene objects and, once, even a motor car. In the 1960s, the college Fellows upstaged them by commissioning the Oxford Architects Partnership to design Brutalist lodgings and a senior common room on either side of the hall. In their case, the offence is more permanent.

Brasenose college

⭐ Tudor college opposite the Radcliffe Camera

Radcliffe Square, Oxford; private house, open all year

Brasenose was, like Queen's, a North Country college. It took its name from the old Brasenose Hall, which had a medieval knocker of a 'brazen nose'. The knocker now resides in the hall, having been retrieved from Stamford in Lincolnshire where it was taken by northern scholars in 1330, following their persecution by Oxford's southerners. The knocker was re-acquired in 1890 by buying the property to which it was attached. There are still Brasenose street names in Stamford.

The college is overshadowed by St Mary's Church, the Radcliffe Camera and the towers of All Souls. Its exterior presents itself to the square in the most delightful way. The college

wall breaks step when it reaches the chapel window, where the crenellation is interrupted by a classical panel, a Gothic window surmount and a broken pediment. This mix of Gothic and classical motifs well reflects Oxford's architectural confusion in the 17th century – as with Hawksmoor's All Souls screen opposite (see page 150).

The Old Quad was begun in 1509, with assertive neo-Tudor dormers added in the 17th century. The more intriguing part of the college lies to the south, the Chapel Quad with, buried on one side the medieval kitchens of the old Brasenose Hall. The chapel was begun under Cromwell and, like its exterior to the square, is a stylistic hybrid. Everywhere here one sees Gothic tracery and classical keystones and pilasters. The chapel has a conventional Oxford T-plan, but with an extraordinary roof, of hammerbeams supporting fan vaults, vividly painted in medieval colours, rising above a classical screen and organ loft. It is dated 1665, when Charles II came to Oxford to escape the plague.

To the south is New Quad, designed in 1887 by the Oxford revivalist T. G. Jackson in a neo-Jacobean style. A less conspicuous impact is made by the early Modernists, Powell & Moya, in their 1960 Platnauer Building, widely regarded as Oxford's best early post-war work. It now looks bleak in its tiny alley west of New Quad.

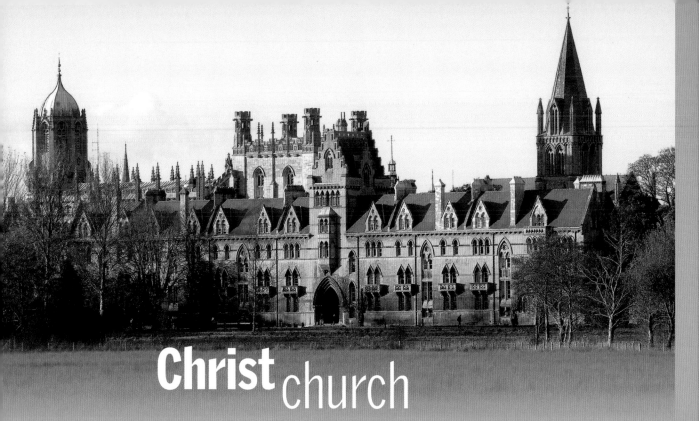

Christ church

★ ★ ★ Wolsey's college with Wren's Tom Tower

St Aldates, Oxford; private house, open all year

Christ Church is the grandest of the Oxford colleges. Wren's Tom Tower vies with Magdalen as symbol of Oxford University as a whole. Tom Quad is the biggest quad and Peckwater the most aristocratic. The hall staircase is the most regal and the art gallery the richest.

The college's founder was Cardinal Wolsey. The Augustinian priory of St Frideswide, dissolved in 1527, was reborn as Cardinal College, with 60 canons, 40 scholars, associated chaplains and servants. With the fall of Wolsey in 1529, Henry VIII retained the foundation as the base for his new Oxford Cathedral. The Latin for Christ Church, *aedes Christi*, gave it the nickname 'the House'.

Christ Church was staunchly Stuart. Charles I made it his Oxford headquarters, indeed his palace, during the Civil War and Tom Quad was his parade ground. Samuel Fell and his son John dominated the college under both Charleses, the latter expelling John Locke for absenteeism and William Penn for lack of orthodoxy. The college survived, recruiting well-born undergraduates and producing more prime ministers than any other institution. As late as the 1960s, rooms in its Canterbury Quad were reserved for those with titles.

Any view of Christ Church starts with Tom Tower, gatehouse of Wolsey's college and like its bell and quad, named after him. Its outside wall to St Aldates is confident and urban, the tower balanced by others on the north and south corners. This assertion of princely supremacy can, on a grey and foggy night, be reminiscent of the Kremlin.

By the time of his fall, Wolsey had built only three sides of Tom Quad. Even Tom Tower was not completed until the Restoration, when Wren designed its upper storey. He warned the Fellows that he would adhere to Gothic, 'to agree with the Founder's work' and to avoid an 'unhandsome medley', but the result 'will necessarily fall short of the beauty of the other way'. Wolsey's original turrets are thus given vertical shafts culminating in ogee caps. Like Hawksmoor's All Souls, Tom Tower appears to be an exercise is stylistic humour.

'The hall staircase is the most regal...'

Tom Quad is clearly unfinished. It was meant to have a cloister, the ghost of the vault forming arches along the façades. Were it not for the Victorian additions of Fell Tower and Bell Tower, the space would seem rather featureless. The Mercury fountain in the middle is a copy of one by Giovanni da Bologna, on a base by Lutyens. Here loutish blue-bloods would soak college weaklings after dinner, to be fined money they could well afford by ever indulgent dons.

To the east of Tom Quad is the cathedral and cloister, a charming backwater that seems detached from college and city alike. On the south side is Wolsey's Great Hall approached by a majestic staircase popularly supposed to be medieval. It is not. The fan vault is of 1640, another Oxford archaism, and the staircase even later, by James Wyatt of 1805. The hall is the largest in Oxford and mostly original, with a hammerbeam roof but later panelling. Its pendants are emphatically Wolsey, as is much of the heraldry, left in place by an apparently tolerant Henry.

There remains Georgian and modern Christ Church. Peckwater Quad was designed in 1705 by the Dean, Henry Aldrich, round three symmetrical sides, beautifully proportioned and with central pediments. It was to house the new breed of Oxford commoners, said to be accustomed to such grand architectural style in their own homes.

The fourth side was completed by another amateur, George Clarke of All Souls, to house the library. This is more in the Baroque tradition, its attached Corinthian columns rising directly from the ground, past boldly pedimented first floor windows to a heavy entablature. The library interior might be the ballroom of a Roman palazzo, with high classical balconies and a delightful Rococo ceiling, including a composition of musical instruments. By the 1960s the library exterior was an astonishing sight, crumbling so badly that chunks of masonry could be removed by hand. It had to be completely refaced.

To the left of the library is the aristocratic seclusion of Canterbury Quad, with a triumphal gate onto Merton Street. Behind is the new Christ Church art gallery by Powell & Moya in 1967, low, minimalist and refreshingly inconspicuous.

'... rooms in its
Canterbury Quad
were reserved for
those with titles.'

Corpus Christi

 Late medieval college with Georgian additions

Merton Street, Oxford; private house, open all year

The college is one of Oxford's smallest and most charming. It was founded at the end of the medieval era in 1517 by Henry VII's Bishop of Winchester, Richard Foxe. It soon became secular under the influence of Foxe's contemporary Bishop of Exeter, Hugh Oldham, who presciently asked, 'Shall we build houses and provide livelihoods for a company of bussing monks, whose end and fall we may ourselves live to see?' Despite its dedication to the late-medieval cult of transubstantiation, the college was a centre of Renaissance education. It taught Greek and its first President, John Claymond, had previously entertained Erasmus when President of Magdalen, and instituted the teaching of ancient Greek at the university.

The Front Quad on Merton Street was built on the site of five old halls. The President lived above the gatehouse, set off-centre next to the hall. The room has a 16th-century heraldic ceiling. The hall retains its hammerbeam roof with carved pendants, designed by Humphrey Coke, Henry VII's master carpenter. Its elaborate panelling, fireplace and William-and-Mary screen were installed by a wealthy President and college benefactor, Edward Turner, after 1700. In the centre of the quad is a pretty sundial with astronomical signs, bequeathed by Charles Turnbull in 1581. The foundation emblem, a pelican in her piety, crowns the obelisk.

The library is essentially Jacobean and, like many in Oxford, retains its early bookshelves. It still possesses 310 of the 371 medieval books catalogued in Elizabeth I's day. Corpus Christi succeeded in hiding its plate during the Civil War, when such wealth was being confiscated by King Charles to pay his troops.

In addition to his work on the hall, Turner had the Oxford master mason, William Townesend, build a new cloister and Fellows' Building beyond the chapel. This charming backwater might be the courtyard of a Palladian house in Venice. The loggia faces a graceful three-storey building, whose outer façade looks out towards Christchurch Meadow.

A small building in the alley between Corpus and Christ Church culminates in the former President's Lodgings, by Michael Powers in 1957. It claims the title of first Modernist building in Oxford.

'The college is **one of** Oxford's **smallest** and most **charming**.'

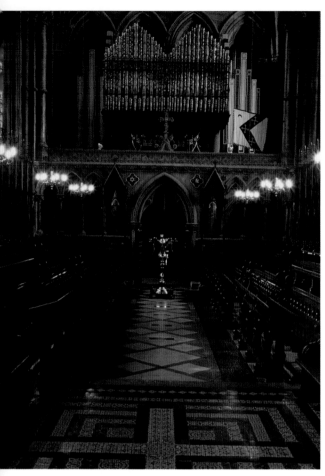

Exeter college

⭐ Medieval college rebuilt in the 17th century

Turl Street, Oxford; private house, open all year

Above George Gilbert Scott's chapel at Exeter was built during the 1850s and finally consecrated on St Luke's Day (October 18th) 1859. The western end of the chapel is dominated by the massive organ gallery. In front of this, in the centre of the aisle, is a lectern in the shape of an eagle. Presented to the college in 1637, it is the only pre-Victorian piece to have been used to furnish the chapel.

Most colleges have some historical link to parts of Britain, now sadly eroded by political correctness. Exeter was for students from Devon and Cornwall, founded in 1314 by the Bishop of Exeter, Walter de Stapledon. The endowment was enhanced by another west countryman, Sir William Petre, in the 16th century.

Like most of the inner colleges based on medieval halls, Exeter rebuilt itself in the Stuart boom of the early 17th century. Only Palmer's Tower in a corner of the front quad survives of the medieval buildings. In 1618 rebuilding began with an entrance on the Turl, not completed until the end of the century. The hall has a magnificent Jacobean screen, the top part salvaged from the old chapel, and fine beams in its open roof.

Exeter's most celebrated building fills the north side of the quad and is unmissable. This is Sir Gilbert Scott's Chapel. The exterior is of banded stone with a lofty flèche turret. Based on the Sainte-Chapelle in Paris, it is a single vaulted chamber, immensely high, with delicate tierceron ribs and Decorated window tracery, Gothic truly 'reaching for Heaven'. A tapestry by Morris and Burne-Jones hangs in a side chapel. This is one of Oxford's best Victorian buildings and makes the surrounding Tudor-Gothic seem tame.

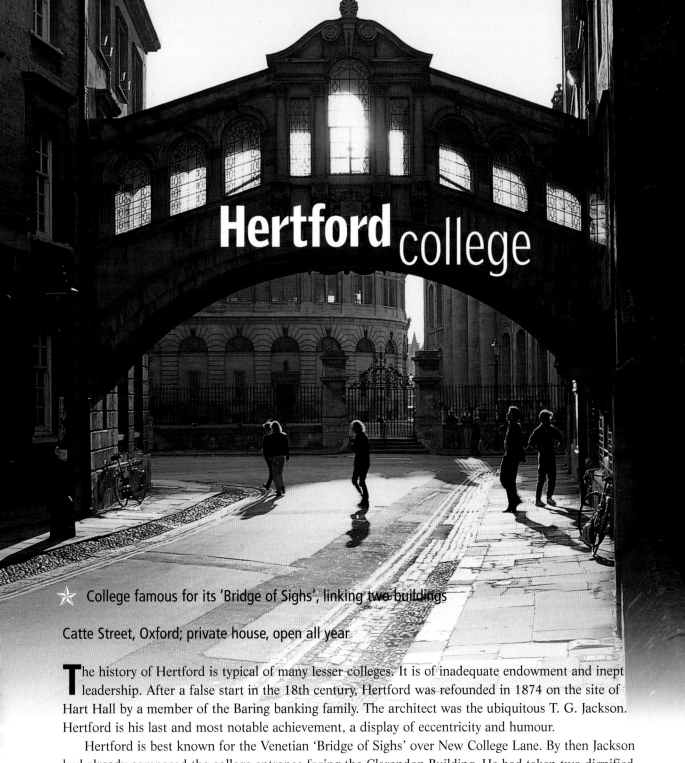

Hertford college

★ College famous for its 'Bridge of Sighs', linking two buildings

Catte Street, Oxford; private house, open all year

The history of Hertford is typical of many lesser colleges. It is of inadequate endowment and inept leadership. After a false start in the 18th century, Hertford was refounded in 1874 on the site of Hart Hall by a member of the Baring banking family. The architect was the ubiquitous T. G. Jackson. Hertford is his last and most notable achievement, a display of eccentricity and humour.

Hertford is best known for the Venetian 'Bridge of Sighs' over New College Lane. By then Jackson had already composed the college entrance facing the Clarendon Building. He had taken two dignified Georgian façades left from Hart Hall and linked them with an entrance worthy of Vanbrugh, with a flourish of Venetian windows. The inside of this block, facing what is called Old Buildings Quad, is adorned with an Oxford original, a spiral staircase borrowed from the French Renaissance Château de Blois. It is extraordinary.

Equally extraordinary is the Bridge of Sighs. This was not erected until 1914, to enable undergraduates to get from the old quad to Hertford's only bathrooms in the new building to the north. Here Jackson decided that the best answer to a 20th-century need lay with the 15th century. As Pevsner remarked, Jackson was an architect 'who knew no fear'. The whole composition is a most charming contribution to the story of English Picturesque, in this case in a style sometimes termed 'Anglo-Jackson'.

Above left Queen Elizabeth I granted Jesus College its first royal charter in 1571; her full-length portrait looks down over the hall. Reputedly by Nicholas Hilliard or his school, the painting was presented to the college in 1687 by a former fellow, James Jeffreys, brother of the infamous Judge Jeffreys.

Jesus college

 College with Elizabethan origins and Jacobean buildings

Turl Street, Oxford; private house, open all year

The college was traditionally Welsh. Although founded under Elizabeth I by Hugh Price, it did not start building until 1617. It was Protestant but Anglican Church of Wales. It had no truck with the Oxford Movement. Half its members were Welsh well into the 20th century, with fellowships for Welsh speakers. In her satirical novel, *The Matter of Wales*, Jan Morris had a victorious Hitler appoint the Principal of Jesus King of Wales.

Jesus is a classic instance of Jacobean Oxford choosing 'any style provided it is Tudor-Gothic'. The corner block between Turl Street and Market Street dates from the 16th century but the remainder of the two main quads were built in the 17th century as and when funds sufficed. They have the familiar Oxford Tudor windows and decorative Dutch gables, crowding the skyline like Welsh dragons' teeth and lightened by exuberant flower boxes.

The hall has 17th-century panelling and a screen with more Welsh dragons. A keen eye can detect dragons even in the fine stucco work. One of the college's three portraits of Elizabeth I hangs over the high table. Jesus library is a delight, with its 17th-century bookcases intact.

Keble college

Parks Road, Oxford; private house, open all year

Is Keble lovely or is it not? For at least a century after its completion, Keble was seen as the epitome of High-Church Victorianism and/or muscular Christian evangelism. It was widely detested as such. How fashion changes.

Keble was founded in 1868, two years after the death of John Keble, founder of the Oxford Movement. It was endowed from public subscription, for poor students entering the priesthood, the first new foundation at Oxford since Wadham in the early 17th century. The commission to design it went to William Butterfield, architect of All Saint's, Margaret Street in London and 'archbishop' of Oxford Tractarianism. His first Oxford work was the modest Balliol Chapel. At Keble, public subscription was enhanced by money for the chapel, library and hall from the Bristol guano tycoon, William Gibbs of Tyntesfield in Somerset. Butterfield had money and to spare.

The college is unlike any other, spacious, generous and as grand as Gothic could be. It is formed of two asymmetrical quads, conventional only in having chapel, hall, library and residential ranges. The rooms were off corridors rather than staircases, cheaper and considered more conducive to college life. Keble undergraduates were assumed to be too poor to need servants.

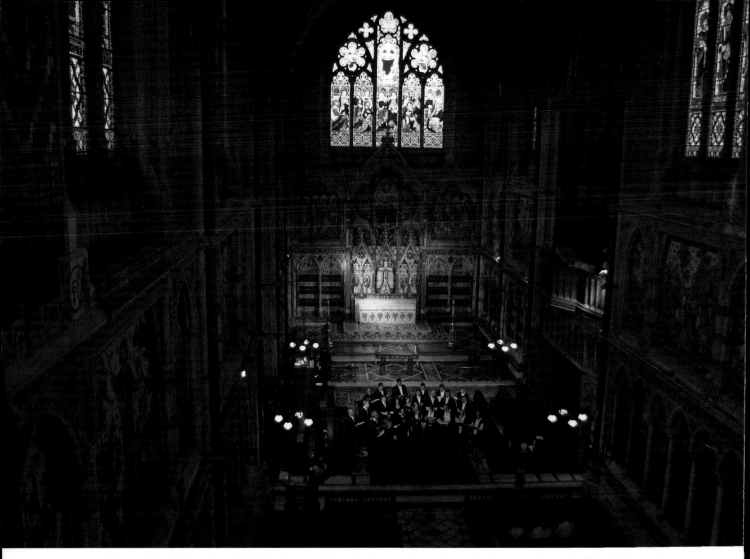

Above Keble College chapel is richly decorated, its walls lined with mosaics depicting scenes from the life of Christ and portrayals of medieval saints and Old Testament prophets. The college's most famous treasure, *The Light of the World*, hangs in a side-chapel, placed there by Butterfield in 1890. Holman Hunt had given the painting to the college some years before, in 1879, on the understanding that it would be displayed in the main body of the Chapel.

Butterfield seemed unmoved by Oxford's traditional Tudor-Gothic or by its sandy limestone. He employed patterned polychrome brick to lozenge-patterned walls below restless gables and turrets. No façade is the same. At Keble, the eye never rests.

Over all towers the chapel, much the biggest in Oxford. It towers as does an abbey church over its cloisters. The whole composition of Keble was intended to point to its chapel, and through it to God. Its height is given added thrust by the quad outside having a sunken lawn and by the nave window sills lying above the quad roofline.

Keble Chapel is Italian Gothic. Its interior height is emphasized by the elevation of the windows above mural-covered walls and by a stupendous high altar. In a side chapel hangs Holman Hunt's painting, *The Light of the World*. Hunt was so furious at the college charging visitors – the porter adding that '*The Light of the World* cannot be seen on Sundays' – that he painted a copy for St Paul's Cathedral in London.

The hall and library are as remarkable as the chapel. Reached by a staircase worthy of an Arthurian film, the two vast chambers are wonders of Victorian design. High Gothic windows light stencilled ceilings and dark panelled walls. The exterior brick and stonework needs regular cleaning. Keble red-and-white is exhilarating. Keble maroon-and-black is grim.

Lincoln college

⭐ Fifteenth-century quad with creeper-clad ranges

Turl Street, Oxford; private house, open all year

Early medieval Oxford was in the Diocese of Lincoln. In 1427, a college was founded by Richard Fleming, eager to counter the reforming influence of the Lollards, Wyclif and others to whom the Church seemed vulnerable. Oxford was always a bastion of tradition. For good measure, Fleming exhumed Wyclif's body and burned it. He desired to protect the Papacy against 'the swinish snouts who presumed to feed upon its precious pearls'. It is ironic that Lincoln educated John Wesley, a son of an orthodox Lincolnshire parson but later scourge of the Anglican church.

Lincoln is a small college on a confined site. The Front Quad retains the character of a 15th-century town house, with hall facing the gatehouse. It is one of my favourite Oxford quads, the Victorian refacing of the ranges concealed by a mass of creeper and window boxes, the latter regarded as the best in Oxford. Old architecture makes its peace with nature. The hall roof is original. Outside is a copy of the Lincoln Imp, a carving on the roof of Lincoln cathedral.

The Jacobean period also saw a new chapel built (after 1608), still Gothic but with superb Renaissance woodwork of cedar, and a barrel vault with decorative motifs. The window glass is painted by Bernard van Linge's studio at its most artistic.

Right The library at Lincoln is unusual in that it is housed in an 18th-century church; the original plasterwork ceiling spans the upper reading room.

Magdalen college

★★★☆ Mid-15th-century college with Georgian range in a deer park

High Street, Oxford; private house, open all year

The tower of Magdalen has defined the city and the University since the Middle Ages. The spread of quadrangles and cloisters between the High and the River Cherwell, backed by an ornamental deer park, epitomizes gracious academic living. Magdalen seems detached from the bustle of Oxford, like an aloof stately home.

The college was the last of the great medieval trio of foundations, after New College and All Souls. Its progenitor was William Waynflete, Bishop of Winchester and Lord Chancellor of England, one of those bishop-statesmen who flourished in pre-Reformation England. He founded his college in 1458 on the site of a hospital for travellers outside the east gate of the city. It was endowed with manors and suppressed priories. Waynflete also founded a grammar school as part of the college.

Magdalen was Oxford's last great project before the Reformation. Its architect was William Orchard, master of late Perpendicular.

'Magdalen **seems detached** from the **bustle** of Oxford, like an **aloof stately home.**'

By 1481 work was sufficiently advanced to receive Edward IV. Erasmus stayed here twenty years later. With space at its disposal, the college never had to rebuild Orchard's work and, as a result, by the 1970s the stone was crumbling to dust. It had to be replaced in its entirety, leading sceptics to reclassify the college façade as c1980. The rebuilding, including replica gargoyles, was immaculate.

Magdalen's bell-tower dominates all, rising direct from the street in four stages and culminating in a chamber of ten bells. From the roof, choristers welcome the dawn on May Day. Entrance to the college is through a tiny door in a gatehouse, as if this were still a medieval hospital. This part of the frontage dates from c1300.

In the front quad is a fragment of Waynflete's old grammar school, facing the magnificent west front of the chapel, with the Founder's Tower acting as ceremonial entrance to the cloister. This is a splendid space, recently repaved and floodlit, the bosses under the tower brilliantly recoloured. The chapel is T-shaped, refurnished in the early 19th century and now hung with the college's great treasure, a contemporary copy of Leonardo's *Last Supper* fresco in Milan.

Beyond lies the Great Quadrangle. Its cloisters do not project into the square but are built into the ground floor of the ranges, with hall, chapel and various towers rising on two sides. This is a supreme work of late-Gothic architecture, with a steep roof and bold battlements. The mythical beasts that 'support' the buttresses form a brilliant gallery of medieval carving.

The hall is original. Renaissance panels depicting Mary Magdalene flank the dais end. The college Fellows process into dinner through a side door across the leads of the

Above The linenfold panelling that lines the 15th-century hall was added in the first half of the 1500s and reputedly came from Reading Abbey after the Dissolution. The carved panels above the high table include scenes from the life of St Mary Magdalene. **Left** The college cloisters retain their 15th-century character, although some of the ranges are not completely original; the north and east cloisters were demolished and rebuilt more than once in the early 19th century.

cloister roof. To perform this feat on a dark autumn night, past windows flickering with candles, is to enjoy a rare reminder of ancient Oxford.

Beyond are the gardens and the Grove, in which sit the Georgian New Buildings. These were designed in 1733 and stretch over 27 bays, seeming to float through the trees on a ground floor loggia. Miles Jebb describes it happily as 'an innocent relic of the Age of Reason placed at a respectful distance from the central glories of the college'. Deer nose at ground floor windows while undergraduates lounge against the loggia walls.

After the dreadful Waynflete Building, erected next to Magdalen Bridge in the 1960s, the college redeemed itself thirty years later with a new lecture theatre and residential block to the north-west by Demetri Porphyrios. The style is part classical, part deferential neo-Tudor, Oxford architecture reinventing its old style with panache.

Merton college

Right Merton's Mob Quad – the origins of its name are obscure – was built at the turn of the 14th century. It houses the world's oldest academic library in continuous use.

★★☆ The oldest college buildings in Oxford

Merton Street, Oxford; private house, open all year

Merton can claim to be the oldest proper college in Oxford or Cambridge. It was pre-eminent from its foundation in 1274 until the arrival of Wykeham's New College over a century later. Walter de Merton rose to be Lord Chancellor. Eager for his many nephews to attend Oxford, he founded a college to house them. The college produced four Archbishops of Canterbury in the succeeding century. For seven centuries, the college bell was rung at 10.30 am every Friday, the time of Walter's accidental drowning in the Medway.

The old gatehouse on Merton Street gives onto a courtyard with the hall opposite. This was the first college building to be constructed for teaching and dining. Although totally rebuilt by Sir Gilbert Scott in the 1870s, it retains its medieval door, coated in swirling ironwork.

The chapel dates from 1290 and has fine Decorated tracery. It was intended to have a nave running across the site of the present Corpus Christi. This was not built, but in 1448 a tower was added, with majestic crossing arches. Its haunting bell sequence chiming the hours is based on Gregorian plainchant.

Above In the antechapel at Merton is a 17th-century memorial to Sir Henry Savile, elected Warden in 1585. An eminent scholar, he became a Fellow of Merton aged just 16 and went on to establish two chairs at the college, one in geometry and the other in astronomy. His monument includes allegorical figures of his academic interests and representations of Merton and Eton – Savile was also Provost of the school, a post he held from 1596.

In 1304 came the two residential ranges attached to the rear of the chapel, now called Mob Quad. Its rooms were originally shared, unheated and had no window glazing. The quad was completed, with its library and treasury, by the 1370s. It has a steep Gothic roof and turret in the north-east corner. The library retains an original stall, with chains for books. Rooms next door are preserved as a memorial to the college's most celebrated Victorian, Max Beerbohm, author of *Zuleika Dobson*, a satire on the impact of women on the all-male University.

The Elizabethan Warden, Henry Savile, had been tutor to the Queen and was a progressive educationist. He founded professorships in mathematics and astronomy and planned Merton's Fellows' Quadrangle next to the hall. The entrance to this quad, the Fitzjames Gateway of 1500, was intended to house queens of England should they visit the university. It is a work of great nobility, with a lierne vault adorned with the signs of the zodiac and other late-Gothic carvings.

The new quad was built in 1610 with, on its far side, a bold Renaissance frontispiece in the form of a 'tower of the orders'. This is a somewhat clumsy precursor of the frontispieces that were later to adorn many college quadrangles, such as William Laud's at St John's. Savile is commemorated in a chapel memorial, attended by Renaissance heroes, Ptolemy, Euclid, Tacitus and others.

New college

✦✦✦ Medieval foundation established round a quad, close by the city walls

New College Lane, Oxford; private house, open all year

No part of Oxford retains the atmosphere of a medieval quartier as does Queen's Lane. High walls flank narrow alleys between old gardens. Over these walls loom stables, smallholdings, secret groves and even farm buildings. Opposite the entrance to New College is a medieval barn. The walls are black and unrestored. This was the defensive architecture of England during the Peasants' Revolt.

New College was founded and built in 1379 by William of Wykeham, son of a Wiltshire peasant and proof that birth was no bar to advancement in pre-Reformation England. As Bishop of Winchester and Chancellor of England, Wykeham sought merit in foundations at Winchester and Oxford, intended for poorer scholars. His 'new' college of seventy fellows housed more than all other Oxford colleges combined. The quad was four times the size of Merton's Mob Quad.

New College was intended as a communal entity in the manner of a monastic house. The area was spacious, land in this part of Oxford being cheap after the Black Death. The Warden's Barn for tithes was built, linked by a bridge (as today) over the lane. The college entrance is at the end of a narrow cul-de-sac beneath a small gatehouse, with statues of the founder and the Virgin Mary in niches over the door.

Inside, lodgings flanked three sides of the 14th-century Great Quad, with chapel and hall filling the fourth side. The quad today is altered from Wykeham's time only by the addition in 1670 of an extra storey, rather spoiling the proportion. The sashes and battlements give it a Gothick appearance.

Above At New College the cloisters, lodgings, chapel and hall are arranged round the quad; this combination, built as a single unit, was an innovation when the college was built in the 1380s and was to become a model for later colleges. Wykeham and his master mason, William Wynford, had already worked together on other projects constructed round central courtyards, most notably at Windsor Castle.

New College chapel with its soaring ante-chapel fills the north-west angle of the quad with a forest of tracery, buttresses and pinnacles. The interior was heavily restored by Sir Gilbert Scott in 1877–81, including a new east reredos like that at All Souls. The choir misericords and medieval glass survive, plus other glass with designs by Reynolds in the west window. Near it stands Epstein's disturbing statue of Lazarus, *Ecce Homo* (1951). To the west of the chapel and in place of a nave is a secret cloister with bell tower. This is a lovely Oxford backwater, a haven little used except for college plays in summer.

The hall is reached by a spectacular staircase with stone lierne vault. The interior was reroofed by Scott and the panelling is 16th century. Beyond the hall are fragments of the old city wall.

A separate passage leads from the Great Quad into the Garden Quad. This was created in the 1680s by a local architect, William Bird, as rooms for gentlemen-commoners. It is a mildly Baroque composition, the façades stepped outwards towards the garden like the backdrop to a rustic theatre. The elevations are full of teasing conceits. The three narrow windows on the inner range become three wide ones on the outer.

A viewing mount was erected in the gardens in 1594, later completed with steps and gazebo. It has now become a wilderness, though bold Fellows occasionally propose to restore its formality.

Nuffield college

⭐ Modern college founded by Oxford's motoring tycoon

New Road, Oxford; private house, open all year

Nuffield requires a sense of humour. The college was founded in 1937 by William Morris, Lord Nuffield (see page 138), creator of the car empire that arose at Cowley, east of the city. Eager to beautify the city's west approach, he bought the old canal basin near the station and proposed a graduate college dedicated to engineering and accountancy be built on the site.

The university old guard was horrified. Nuffield was duly persuaded by the Vice-Chancellor, A. D. Lindsay, to widen his vision to embrace the social sciences generally, but further argument now surrounded the design of the college.

The university selected as architect the little-known Austen Harrison, who had worked mostly in the Mediterranean. His original design was for a Levantine college with flat roofs, blank exteriors and no spire. Morris was a generous man but old-fashioned and precise in the object of his benefaction. He wanted a 'traditional design' and refused otherwise to give a penny.

Compromise was achieved only after the Second World War when Harrison conceded pitched roofs, tiles, gables and dormers, all in Cotswold stone. He even added a 'dreaming spire', which Morris insisted be the highest in Oxford. Two quads are linked by a flight of steps, with pools, almost puddles, in their centres, relics of Harrison's 'Mediterranean'. The hall lies at the head of the main axis, emphasized with a Tudor oriel window. The hall has concrete arches and a red roof.

The tower is at best ungainly. It is used to house the library and rises without modulation to a weak spire. Pevsner claimed that it had a touch of Lutyens about it and 'will, I prophesy, one day be loved'. I doubt it. Vegetation is its best hope, as for the rest of Nuffield. Cotswold revival should be an affectionate style, but is not here. A small chapel in the roof has abstract stained glass by John Piper and Patrick Reyntiens.

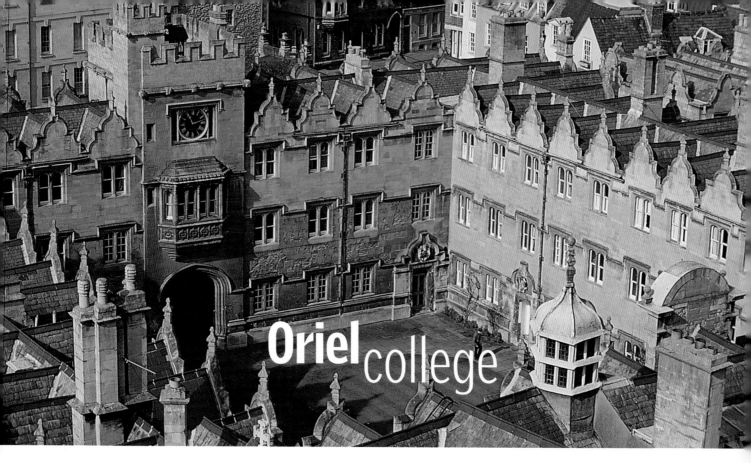

Oriel college

★★ Jacobean rebuilding of a medieval foundation

Oriel Square, Oxford; private house, open all year

The college is named after the oriel window that adorns its façade. It was founded in the early 14th century, in honour of Edward II, a king who might qualify as the first of Oriel's many lost causes. Once the staunchest defenders of the Stuart ascendancy, it was a cradle of Anglo-Catholicism in the 19th century and the last college to admit women, in 1984.

The college grew by acquiring a series of old residential halls between Merton Street and the High. In 1619 it did a clean sweep, rebuilding them all by 1642. The Royalist style employed the customary Oxford gables with Renaissance touches.

This is best exemplified by the spectacular composition of the hall and chapel, directly facing the entrance. Six large traceried windows fill the façade, culminating in two Tudor-style bay windows. The central porch, reached up a splendid sweep of steps, announces that Charles I was reigning at the time it was built. The whole is anachronistically surmounted by a classical gable. The symmetry of the range conceals a traditional medieval plan. The hall is off-centre behind the porch and has a screens passage. It has the last hammerbeam roof to be built in Oxford.

Oriel's Back Quad is a place of trees and creeper, setting for James Wyatt's fine library façade of 1789. Here Wyatt is in classical mode. He built it above a 'common room' in the space below, the first such room in Oxford. It was here that the Anglo-Catholic Oxford Movement took root, with John Henry Newman, John Keble, Edward Pusey and Richard Froude. Oriel also saw the early application of the tutorial system, one-to-one supervision of undergraduate work.

To the north lies St Mary's Quad, relic of St Mary's Hall added to the college in 1902. It is a picturesque jumble of buildings, dominated by Basil Champneys' 1908 Rhodes Building, a throwback to the style of the Front Quad, complete with a Dutch Renaissance gatehouse on the High. This is no longer used.

Pembroke college

⭐ Jacobean college with Victorian hall and Georgian chapel

St Aldates, Oxford; private house, open by arrangement

Pembroke is the unknown college. Tucked away behind St Aldate's church, it can seem little more than a supplicant outside the gates of Christ Church opposite. It was founded in 1624 with funds provided by an Oxfordshire maltster and a Shropshire clergyman. At Pembroke, named after the university chancellor of the day, these funds never seemed sufficient. The college's most distinctive alumnus was Dr Johnson, but he left after a year.

Pembroke has a pleasant Old Quad, of intimate and unadorned 17th-century ranges, refaced by the Victorians. Beyond, a passage leads to the noble Chapel Quad. This is dominated by a Victorian Gothic hall of 1846 by John Hayward, lofty with a hammerbeam roof and reached up a long flight of steps. To the south, after a break for a garden, is the chapel. The classical exterior is by the Oxford Georgian builder, William Townesend. The interior was completely redecorated in 1884 by C. E. Kempe and is one of his most dazzling works, in High Renaissance style and with a glorious painted ceiling. It alone is worth visiting Pembroke to see.

The Queen's college

★★ College with classical façade, inspired by French architecture

High Street, Oxford; private house, open by arrangement

Queen's is the centrepiece of the view up the High towards St Mary's. So stately is its appearance that few realize how alien is its form, that of a French *cour d'honneur*. Such is Oxford's diversity that it seems perfectly in place.

The first queen was Philippa, wife of Edward III, and succeeding queens consort have been *ex officio* patrons. The early college offered places for scholars from Cumberland specifically and from other northern counties, a tradition that lasted until stopped by political correctness at the end of the 20th century. The college was much given to medieval ceremony, with costumes for Fellows and choristers, a trumpet for dinner and a horn loving-cup. The original college was housed in a warren of medieval inns and halls at the junction of the High and Queen's Lane. At the end of the 17th century, a bequest from Sir Joseph Williamson enabled a complete rebuilding, assisted by Wren and enhanced by the later patronage of Queen Caroline, wife of George III. Her statue occupies the cupola on the High.

Queen's is the finest classical building in Oxford. The Front Quad, begun in 1709, was said to have been inspired by Hawksmoor but designed by the amateur Oxford architect, George Clarke of All Souls, and by the builder, William Townesend. The inspiration was allegedly the Palais de Luxembourg in Paris. The concept of an open screen to enclose a front courtyard is indeed Parisian, though one which Hawksmoor employed shortly afterwards in his new quad at All Souls. Despite its alien style and aloof façade, the screen and indeed the whole façade contrive to elevate the character of this superb street.

Above left Queen's chapel, consecrated in 1719, was once thought to have been by Sir Christopher Wren, because of its similarity to his library at Trinity College Cambridge; it is now believed to be the work of Henry Aldrich. The west gallery houses an organ made by the Danish firm, Frobenius, which was installed in 1965. **Above right** The library at Queen's was built at the end of the 17th century after the college was endowed with the book collection of Bishop Thomas Barlow, Provost of Queen's from 1658 to 1677.

The Front Quad was completed by 1734. The central block is severely classical, with a portico and cupola echoing that of the loggia arcades beneath. The hall has a lofty classical interior with sweeping barrel vault and high windows. The chapel is likewise classical with plasterwork worthy of a City of London church. The ceiling roundel is by Sir James Thornhill, no less.

Townesend seems to have been left to complete the North Quad himself. Its east range conceals an earlier range by Wren, now visible only from Queen's Lane outside. Opposite is the magnificent library designed in 1692 by one of Oxford's many architectural dons, Dean Henry Aldrich of Christ Church's Peckwater Quad. The loggia below was once open, as at Wren's Trinity Library in Cambridge. Above runs a serene 11-bay façade worthy of an Austrian palace, its pediment surmounted by what looks like an imperial eagle.

The library interior is as much banqueting hall as library. High windows illuminate swirling Rococo plasterwork in the ceiling panels, by Thomas Roberts, an outstanding local craftsman responsible for the ceilings at Rousham Park. The bookcases are open and spacious, beautifully crafted, a contrast with the cramped stacks of their Jacobean precursors. They speak of the world of Wren, Newton and Locke, defying the introverted closets of the medieval schoolmen.

St Catherine's college

As 20th-century Oxford architecture, St Catherine's is everything Nuffield is not. After Nuffield we need a pint of beer. After St Catherine's we need a sauna. Nuffield's patron sought consolation in the past, and failed to find it. St Catherine's was meant to evoke a socialist academic utopia. It was the creation of its first Master, Lord Bullock, yet it could hardly be farther removed from the personality of this down-to-earth, bangers-and-mash character. For some reason Lord Bullock thought being modern meant Scandinavian.

St Catherine's Society had been formed in 1868 for poor students unable to afford the cost of college membership. It became a full college in 1962 and needed a proper building. Bullock went on a tour to find an architect appropriate for his vision. He decided on the Dane, Arne Jacobsen, 'from the moment I walked into [his] Munkegaards School' near Copenhagen. The plan is ruthlessly geometric. It pays no respect to the curve of the adjacent Cherwell River, or to any curve at all. The only curved thing is the bicycle shed which greets visitors at the entrance, and a fine bronze by Hepworth.

The most pertinent comment on St Catherine's is that nobody has ever imitated it. Usually photographed through a thick Cherwell mist, its parallelograms disappear to infinity. Its harsh concrete and steel have not softened with age. The rooms are as hard inside as outside, divorced from the world behind sheets of water and glass. Jacobsen designed everything, even the spoons. It seems an offence to move so much as an armchair from its dominant right angle. This is truly the architect as dictator.

St Catherine's minimalist asceticism engendered much debate. The critic, Reyner Banham, called it the 'best motel in Oxford'. Pevsner, the college's most enthusiastic celebrant, remarked that if young people did not like the college 'that may be an argument against them rather than the college'. He felt it embodied architectural discipline against youthful 'self-permissiveness'. That says it all.

St Edmund hall

★ Small-scale college with Baroque library building

Queen's Lane, Oxford; private house, open all year

This tiny, charming college must be inhabited by Hobbits. It was the last surviving non-collegiate academic hall in Oxford. Most were merged with colleges in the 19th century, St Edmund's joining with neighbouring Queen's. It finally won independent collegiate status in 1957, keeping hall in its title in deference to history. Its nickname is Teddy Hall.

The college is essentially one quad with modern insertions behind. An unobtrusive entrance to the street leads to a tiny picturesque courtyard with a disused well in the centre and a robinia tree. The hall is next to the entrance, the size of a modest dining room.

At the far side of the quad is the old library, an eccentric essay in Oxford Baroque, designed by a local mason in 1682. A quaint Ionic portico rises two storeys to a pediment containing a small bell. The columns appear to be an afterthought, given how they crowd out the windows. A lesser pediment over the door rests on piles of books. Beneath the library is a lobby to the equally small chapel, a charming 17th-century chamber with windows by Burne-Jones and a pretty Flemish triptych.

The rest of Front Quad is 20th-century reproduction Tudor. Through an arch to the north is a path across the churchyard of the former Norman church of St Peter-in-the-East, now the library. The whole group is a delicious backwater in the heart of Oxford.

Less happy are the new buildings which were crammed beyond the Front Quad in 1968, by the local firm of Kenneth Stevens. Walls are of stone and shuttered concrete. The upper storeys attempt to repeat the gables and chimneys of the Front Quad, flanking them with a lift tower in concrete.

'This tiny, **charming** college must be **inhabited** by **Hobbits.**'

St John's college

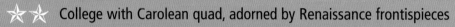

✦✦ College with Carolean quad, adorned by Renaissance frontispieces

St Giles, Oxford; private house, open all year

Just when Oxford seems to dissolve into suburb up the wide thoroughfare of St Giles, St John's appears, spread comfortably along its right-hand flank.

The medieval Front Quad was mostly built by Archbishop Chichele in 1437, as a Cistercian college dedicated to St Bernard, whose statue guards the gatehouse. The college was unfinished at the Dissolution and was refounded by Thomas White during the Marian Counter-Reformation in 1555. A City merchant, White was Roman Catholic and required his college 'to strengthen the orthodox faith'. He dedicated it

to St John as patron of tailors and endowed it with extensive land north of the city. This land has been the basis of the college's wealth.

On the gatehouse is a fine Eric Gill statue of St John the Baptist. The Front Quad embraces the hall, chapel and President's lodgings, all dating from White's refoundation. None is special, although the Buttery is said to be a survival of the old Cistercian buildings. The hall screen is by James Gibbs. William Townesend's massive hall fireplace generated so much heat – I recall as an undergraduate at the college – that nobody could sit near it.

St John's glory is Canterbury Quad. White's Fellows were to study theology to counter

Lutheran and Calvinist heresy and the college remained a bastion of the Stuart Counter-Reformation. William Laud was President from 1611 to 1621 and later Archbishop to Charles I. He built this quadrangle in 1631. His entertainment of the King here in 1636 was said to have cost as much as the quad itself. Laud adapted the old medieval library, but built new ranges to the east and west, crowning them with Renaissance frontispieces dedicated to the King and his queen, Henrietta Maria.

These frontispieces are among the jewels of Oxford. They address each other across the grass, man and wife in dignified conversation. The classical orders are simple, two tiers, one Doric the other Ionic, but the bases are elongated, adorned with cartouches and drapes. The niche statues are by the French sculptor, Le Sueur, also responsible for the equestrian statue of Charles I in London's Trafalgar Square.

The two ranges are set on classical loggias, but above them the Middle Ages survive in the form of rude battlements and grotesque corbel heads. The old religion needed the last architectural word.

The library is Elizabethan, L-shaped round the corner of the quad. It still has its ancient cases, shelves and seats, some looking out over the college's fine gardens. The North Quad contains the controversial 'beehives' by the Architects' Co-Partnership in 1958. These curious rooms were among the earliest Modernist buildings in Oxford, deliberately eschewing the prevailing Oxford stone. They have not worn well.

To the north of the old college is the Thomas White Quadrangle by Arups in 1975, its Brutalist concrete offset by white stone turrets containing staircases. Beyond is an excellent work of the 1990s, the Garden Quad by Richard MacCormac, Oxford's most successful variation on a quadrangle theme. Staircase pavilions, classical in form but not in detail, are set round a Piranesian well. This is brilliantly lit at night, and by day offers a Mediterranean play of light and darkness on its colonnades.

Trinity college

 Tudor college with Oxford's first classical chapel

Broad Street, Oxford; private house, open all year

Trinity is oddly unobtrusive. It was founded in 1555, the same year as St John's, on the site of an existing Benedictine hall called Durham College. Its founder was Sir Thomas Pope, Henry VIII's Treasurer, and linked to Magdalene College, Cambridge. Like Magdalene, it became fashionable among the lesser county aristocracy. During the Civil War it was captured by Colonel Ireton, himself of Trinity, surely the only man to have literally taken his old college by storm.

The college is best known for its gates on Broad Street, designed in 1737 and a more stylish face to the world than Oxford's usual wall of Cotswold stone. A range of quaint 17th-century cottages forms the actually entrance. They were saved from demolition in the 19th century by a letter from William Morris to the *Daily News*. Inside the front garden and partly masked by cedars and catalpas are two Victorian ranges of 1883, by T. G. Jackson in a laboured neo-Dutch style. Behind them is the modern Cumberbatch Quad, a terrible mess.

The true entrance to the college is beneath its chapel tower. The architect is unknown, although the ubiquitous Sir Christopher Wren is thought to have approved the design. Dating from 1691, it was the first Oxford chapel in the classical style (yet a quarter-century after Wren's Pembroke Chapel in Cambridge). Four arched windows with Corinthian pilasters are offset by a fine tower topped by statues of Geometry, Medicine, Astronomy and Theology. Inside is the finest Baroque reredos in Oxford. The swags are possibly by Grinling Gibbons, set in a wonderful array of woodwork and plasterwork.

Above The late 17th-century chapel at Trinity may have been designed by Henry Aldrich, Dean of Christ Church, but it is believed that the college also consulted Sir Christopher Wren. The carved woodwork behind the altar is regarded as the work of Grinling Gibbons and is composed of five different types of wood: pear, lime, juniper, oak and walnut.

Beyond lies Durham Quad, the east range dating from the old Durham College of c1417. To the left is the Jacobean hall of 1618, still with a medieval bay window, redecorated in the 18th century. The Garden Quad to the north completes the sequence. Two sides of this quad were by Wren in 1665, but his work was altered to conform to a Georgian wing added in 1802. Here again we see Oxford's genius for three-sided courtyards facing gardens or country.

The garden was originally a formal parterre culminating in more fine gates onto Park Road. This was destroyed by the Victorian craze for naturalism. It should be restored.

University college

⭐ College with Tudor-Gothic style quads

High Street, Oxford; private house,
open by arrangement

University College is an architectural curiosity. It was formed by William of Durham to support a dozen scholars in 1249. Its fortunes waxed and waned (mostly waned) until, like many colleges, it found the energy to redevelop its mixed bag of properties on the High in the early 17th century. Later John Radcliffe, physician to William III, endowed the completion of the work, adding University College to his benefactions to the Camera and the Infirmary.

Two quads form the core of the college, their outer walls backing onto the High. The Front Quad was begun in 1634, in the Anglo-Dutch style. Hall and chapel are back-to-back along the south side of the quad. After many vicissitudes, the hall saw its hammerbeam roof reinstated facsimile in 1904. The second quad of 1719, on Radcliffe's express wishes, imitated the style of the first. This hardly made for innovation, qualifying as Gothic revival revival. There is even fan-vaulting under the gatehouse. Radcliffe appears in a niche, with his doctor's emblems of rod and snake.

In the chapel is a memorial by Flaxman depicting the naturalist, Sir William Jones, taking notes from Red Indians. More extraordinary is the Shelley Memorial in its own mausoleum. This flamboyant undergraduate was expelled for atheism and indiscipline in 1811, yet is commemorated in a quasi-religious shrine. The memorial was designed by Basil Champneys in 1892. The sculpture by Onslow Ford is of a naked youth lying on a slab supported by the mourning Muse of Poetry. It is a surreal Oxford relic.

Below Edward Onslow Ford's marble sculpture for the Shelley Memorial at University College is a representation of the dead poet, washed up on the Italian coast near Viareggio. Shelley had drowned in July 1822 while sailing his schooner, the *Don Juan*, between Livorno and Lerici.

Wadham college

Parks Road, Oxford; private house, open all year

My first experience of Wadham was as a schoolboy applying for entrance. I was put in a freezing attic with a damp bed up a winding staircase. The building, which backed onto Blackwell Street, might well have been condemned as uninhabitable. Mercifully, it has since become one of the college's most harmonious new quads, an informal urban space behind the houses of the old street.

The college was not medieval. It was founded in the academically fertile reign of James I by the widow of a Somerset man, Nicholas Wadham. She never visited Oxford, but presided over its creation from her West Country home. Wadham was another Oxford patron to regard the medieval plan and the Tudor-Gothic style as the only one appropriate for a seat of academic learning. The college was built between 1610 and 1613, with nothing added until the late 20th century.

The Front Quad is of three storeys, each side symmetrical, with chapel and hall filling the far range. Between them is a frontispiece, a 'tower of the orders' as at Merton, with James I and the Wadhams filling the niches. The hall is original, with high hammerbeam roof and openwork pendants. At the time of its construction, there was even an open central hearth, not replaced until as late as 1826. This was surely carrying medievalism to extremes. The smoke louvre in the roof survives.

Wadham shared that fate of many Oxford colleges, with new buildings of the 1970s and 80s partly redeemed by later work of the 1990s. The old gardens now contain a library in incongruous black glass and shuttered concrete by Gillespie, Kidd and Coia. A new quad has been formed next to it from a group of 1950s buildings. Overlooking them is a work by the best of Oxford's recent architects, Richard MacCormac. The Bowra Building comprises a series of staircases and oriel windows leading off an internal street. This is picturesquely aligned to the tower of New College. The materials are properly Oxonian, mostly stone, and each element of the design has its own personality, a doorway, step or vista.

Worcester college

★★ Medieval college with
Hawksmoor range

Worcester Street, Oxford; private
house, open all year

Worcester is a college out on a limb.
It sits at the end of Beaumont
Street on the site of a former
Benedictine foundation of 1283 called
Gloucester College. The site was
acquired by Sir Thomas White, founder
of St John's, under Mary I and renamed
Gloucester Hall. It languished for two
centuries but was refounded in 1714
under the endowment of Sir Thomas
Cookes, whose Worcestershire estates
led to the change in name.

The new Worcester was an event in
Oxford architectural circles. Many
offered plans, but the assiduous
Hawksmoor appears to have won,
collaborating with the All Souls
amateur, George Clarke. Their intention
was for an H-shaped, classical building
facing open country beyond. Money was
short and only one range on the far side
was completed, producing the
picturesquely lop-sided Main Quad of
today. A range of 15th-century buildings
from the old Gloucester College was left
standing, with a medieval yard behind.

The main façade of Worcester
towards Beaumont Street is the front of
the H, containing the hall and chapel,
both culminating in bold Venetian
windows. From the quad, Hawksmoor's
block is a serene composition with deep
eaves, large windows and shadows in
the loggia beneath. The hall was
decorated by James Wyatt in the 1780s.
His decoration of the chapel was swept
aside by William Burges in 1864. The

Right According to Pevsner, Burges did not completely obliterate Wyatt's work at Worcester chapel, 'but he swamped it'. Wyatt's simple classical interior was covered with every conceivable form of decoration. Burges even incorporated humour in his scheme; the text of the *Te Deum* was inlaid into the pews so that the word 'God' appeared over the Provost's stall.

High Victorian Burges called Wyatt's work the 'vilest Renaissance of George III's time'. His replacement is astonishing, a riot of birds, animals, mosaics and wall paintings by Henry Holiday, Oxford's best Victorian interior.

The arches of the loggia are repeated blind on the residential north side of the quad. This range culminates in the Provost's Lodgings of 1773, a handsome Palladian house, designed by Henry Keene. Its garden front rises three storeys above a basement, with a fine double staircase down to the lawn. The stone is a golden Cotswold.

The old medieval range crouches on the south side of the quad, as if cowering before the impending demolition. It is not a complete range, like Merton's Mob Quad (see page 167), but a row of distinct houses, known as *camerae*, each one for scholars sponsored by a different monastery and with the relevant monastic emblem above its door. Behind the range is the tiny Pump Quad, fashioned from two more *camerae*. Here one can see the old chimney flue of the medieval kitchen.

The south side of Worcester contains some of Oxford's worst modern buildings and one of its best. The latter is on the far side of the lake, another work by the ubiquitous Richard MacCormac, built in 1984. It is like a Frank Lloyd Wright set in a Japanese water garden, yet with an Oxford urbanity. No two rooms are the same.

Glossary

The aim in this book has been to avoid terms not familiar to the lay person. However, some specialist terms in common use in architectural circles may have crept in, for which the following may be helpful.

acanthus – pattern of an exotic Mediterranean flower with large leaves used in classical decoration.

anthemion – a honeysuckle flower pattern used in classical decoration.

Artisan Mannerist – buildings created by masons using pattern books (rather than architects) in the period c.1615–75. Mannerism originated in 16th-century Italy and was characterised by Classical elements used in unusual ways. It was taken up in the Low Countries, then spread to England.

ashlar – block of masonry fashioned into a wall, either load-bearing or to cover brick.

bailey, inner and outer – a fortified enclosure, usually moated and surrounded by a curtain wall, containing a motte (mound) with a keep on top. Walls are topped by battlements, with crenellations which protected defenders from arrows, and machicolations, or floor openings, through which attackers could be fired down on.

baluster – upright post supporting the handrail on stairs.

bargeboard – wooden board protecting the eaves of a roof.

bay – a space of wall between any vertical element, such as an upright beam, pillar or a division into a window or door.

bay window – window projecting out from a flat wall, either canted if the sides are straight, or bowed if curved.

bolection mould – moulding concealing the join of vertical and horizontal surfaces, shaped like an S in cross-section.

Boulle – elaborate inlay work on the surface of furniture, customary in 17th and 18th-century French work.

bow – see bay window

canted – see bay window

cartouche – frame for a picture or statue, often oval and surrounded by a scroll.

caryatid – a column in the shape of a draped female figure.

casements – see sashes

castle of enclosure – a form of early medieval castle in which individual buildings are enclosed within a curtain wall, in contrast to later medieval castles that consisted of a tower with subsidiary buildings in a courtyard to front or rear.

chinoiserie – a style of Rococo with Chinese motifs, often linked with Gothick.

coffering – a ceiling composed of beams enclosing sunken square or round panels.

collars – see roof timbers

corbel – a stone or wood projection in a wall that supports a beam, statue or sill.

cornice – (1) a ledge or projecting upper part of a classical entablature. (2) Moulding at the top of a wall concealing the join with the ceiling.

cottage ornée – late-Georgian/Victorian picturesque cottage, usually with thatched roof and Gothic windows.

crenellation – see bailey

crocket – Gothic decorative device, usually a cusp or curling leaf, at regular intervals on outer edges of spires, pinnacles and gables

cruck – a simple structure of two, usually curved, trunks of wood formed into an inverted V which support the walls and roof of a medieval house.

curtain wall – in castle-building, a wall constructed between defensive projections such as bastions.

dentil – one of a series of small square blocks along the base of a cornice

dorter – a sleeping room or dormitory, especially in a college or monastery.

dressing – a general term for finishings; stone is dressed to either a smooth or ornamental surface.

enfilade – a line of rooms in sequence along one side of a house, usually with interconnecting doors.

entablature – a feature of classical architecture comprising everything above column height, formally composed of architrave, frieze and cornice.

flatwork – decorative plaster or woodwork in low relief.

frontispiece – a decorative bay above a doorway in a Tudor or Jacobean building, customarily composed of Renaissance motifs.

gable – the triangular end of a double-pitched roof, sometimes with stepped or scrolled (Dutch) sides.

garderobe – privy or lavatory, usually discharging into a ditch or moat outside a medieval house.

Great Chamber – see solar

grisaille – monochrome painting, usually a mural and in shades of grey.

grotesque – decorative wall motif of human figures, as found in Roman grottoes.

half-timbering – term for timber-framed house derived from the practice of splitting logs in half to provide beams.

hipped roof – a roof with a sloping end instead of an end gable.

Ho-Ho bird – chinoiserie motif associated with 18th-century Rococo style.

jetty or jettied floor – upper floor extended, or oversailed, beyond the lower one to give more space upstairs and protect lower walls from adverse weather. Jettying also uses the downward thrust of the upper walls to form a cantilever, preventing internal ceiling beams from bowing.

keep – see bailey

king post – see roof timbers

linenfold – a pattern on wall panels imitating folded linen.

louvre – a covered turret above a medieval hall that allowed smoke to escape.

machicolation – see bailey

mannerism – see Artisan Mannerist

mansard – a roof with two separate pitches of slope.

motte – see bailey

mullion – central divider of window, made of metal or stone.

oversail – see jetty

oriel – an upper window projecting from a wall, sometimes (incorrectly) used to indicate a tall medieval window lighting the dais end of the Great Hall.

Palladian – a style of classical architecture, formal and refined outside, often lavish inside, named after Italian architect, Andrea Palladio (1508–80). Moving spirit behind most English classical designers, especially Inigo Jones and, later, Lord Burlington, William Kent and the early Georgians.

parlour – see solar

piano nobile – the main ceremonial floor of a classical building, sitting on the basement or 'rustic' lower floor.

pier-glass – a wall mirror supported by a small table, bracket or console.

pietra dura – literally 'hard stone'; a decorative inlay using highly polished stones such as marble, jasper and porphyry

pilaster – a flat column projecting only slightly from a wall.

pointing – mortar or cement used to seal between bricks.

porte-cochère – a grand porch with a driveway through it, allowing passengers to alight from carriages under cover.

prodigy house – a large, ostentatious house of the Elizabethan/Jacobean period.

putti – unwinged sculptures of chubby boys found in Classical and Baroque decoration.

queen post – see roof timbers

quoins – dressed corner stones.

render – a covering of stucco, cement or limewash on the outside of a building.

Rococo – the final phase of Baroque style in the 18th century, typified by refined painted and plaster decoration, often asymmetrical and with figures.

roof timbers – a tie-beam runs horizontally across the roof space; a king post rises vertically from the tie beam to the apex of the roof; queen posts rise not to the apex but to subsidiary beams known as collars; wind-braces strengthen the roof rafters.

rustic – a name given in Palladian architecture to the lower floor or basement, beneath the piano nobile.

rustication – treatment of ashlar by deep-cutting joints so they look stronger or cruder.

sashes – windows opening by rising on sash ropes or cords, as opposed to casements which open on side hinges.

scagliola – composition of artificial stone that imitates appearance of grained marble.

screens passage – accessed from the main door of a medieval building and built into one end of a Great Hall to shield it from draughts. Door ors arches lead from the passage into the hall on one side and kitchens on other. Above is usually a minstrels' gallery.

Serlian – motifs derived from pattern books of the Italian Renaissance architect, Sebastiano Serlio (1475–1554).

sgraffito – plaster decoration scratched to reveal another colour beneath.

solar – the upstairs room at the family end of a medieval hall, originally above an undercroft or parlour. Originally accessed by ladder or spiral stairs, it was usually replaced by a Great Chamber in the Tudor era.

strapwork – strap or ribbon-like decorative scrolls in Elizabethan and Jacobean design.

stucco – plaster, usually protective, covering for brick, sometimes fashioned to look like stone.

studding – vertical timbers laid close to each other to strengthen the wall. Close-studding tends to indicate wealth.

tie-beam – see roof timbers

undercroft – a vaulted room or crypt beneath a building, partly or wholly underground

vault – a ceiling, usually of stone composed of arches.

Venetian window – Palladian window composed of three components, the centre one arched.

wind-braces – see roof timbers

Simon Jenkins' sources

The best guides to any house are the people who occupy it. They have felt its walls and sensed its seasons. They stand witness to its ghosts, real and imagined, and have thus become part of its history. As a substitute, guidebooks vary widely from the academic to the plain childish. The best are published by English Heritage, erudite and enjoyable. National Trust guidebooks are at last moving from the scholarly to the accessible, and the Trust's compendium *Guide*, by Lydia Greeves and Michael Trinick, is excellent.

My selection of a thousand properties derives from numerous sources. These include Hudson's *Historic Houses and Gardens*, supplemented by *Museums and Galleries* published by Tomorrow's Guides. The Historic Houses Association website is another invaluable source. Of recent house surveys, the best are John Julius Norwich's *Architecture of Southern England* (1985), John Martin Robinson's *Architecture of Northern England* (1986) and Hugh Montgomery-Massingberd's *Great Houses of England and Wales* (2000). Nigel Nicolson's *Great Houses of Britain* (1978) describes the most prominent. Their lists are not exhaustive and include houses not open to the public. Behind them stands Nikolaus Pevsner's massive 'Buildings of England' series, which deals with houses more generously (with plans) in the newer revised editions.

On English domestic architecture, the classics are hard to beat. They include Olive Cook's *The English House Through Seven Centuries* (1968), Alec Clifton-Taylor's *The Pattern of English Building* (1972), Hugh Braun's *Old English Houses* (1962), Sacheverell Sitwell's *British Architects and Craftsmen* (1964) and Plantagenet Somerset Fry's *Castles of Britain and Ireland* (1980).

On specific periods the best are Mark Girouard's *Robert Smythson and the English Country House* (1983), Giles Worsley's *Classical Architecture in England* (1995), Kerry Downes's *English Baroque Architecture* (1966) and Girouard's *The Victorian Country House* (1971). Joe Mordaunt Crook takes a lively look at the Victorian battle of the styles in *The Dilemma of Style* (1989). Jeremy Musson describes the manorial revival in *The English Manor House* (1999) and Gavin Stamp takes a wider look at the same period in *The English House 1860–1914* (1986). *Edwardian Architecture*, edited by Alastair Service (1975), brings the story into the 20th century and Clive Aslet's *The Last Country Houses* (1982) almost completes it.

On social history, Girouard's *Life in the English Country House* (1978) is incomparable. *Creating Paradise* (2000) by Richard Wilson and Alan Mackley sets the house in its economic context. So does Mordaunt Crook's *The Rise of the Nouveaux Riches* (1999) and David Cannadine's *The Decline and Fall of the British Aristocracy* (1990). Adrian Tinniswood offers a fascinating insight in his *History of Country House Visiting* (1989). The desperate post-war bid to save houses is described in Marcus Binney's *Our Vanishing Heritage* (1984) and John Cornforth's *The Country Houses of England 1948–1998* (1998). Peter Mandler covers the same period in his scholarly *The Fall and Rise of the Stately Home* (1997).

Biographies of architects are too legion to list but Howard Colvin's *Biographical Dictionary of British Architects* (1978) was my bible over disputed dates and attributions. Of a more personal character is James Lees-Milne's delightful account of the National Trust's early acquisitions in *People and Places* (1992). Houses in distress are visited in John Harris's *No Voice from the Hall* (1998). *Writers and their Houses* (1993) is a first-class collection of essays, edited by Kate Marsh.

I am indebted to the many architectural commentaries in *Country Life*, champion of the historic buildings cause for over a century. I do not believe I could have found a thousand houses for my list were it not for its progenitors, Edward Hudson and Christopher Hussey, and their many successors.

Contact details

Note: Readers are advised to check opening times before visiting, either via the websites and addresses below or in Hudson's Historic Houses & Gardens, the annual guide to castles, houses and heritage sites open to the public. Houses sited close to the border of a neighbouring county may have that county given as their postal address.

Abingdon: Long Alley Almshouses – St Helen's Churchyard, Abingdon. For information on viewing and open days, contact The Clerk, Christ's Hospital of Abingdon, 1 Old Station Yard, Abingdon, OX14 3LQ www.ch-of-abingdon.org Tel 01235 526487

Abingdon: Merchant's House – 26a East St Helen Street, Abingdon, Oxfordshire www.oxfordpreservation.org.uk Open by arrangement with the Oxford Preservation Trust; tel 01865 242918

All Souls College – High Street, Oxford, Oxfordshire, OX1 4AL www.visitoxford.org & www.all-souls.ox.ac.uk Tel 01865 279379 Contact the college for visiting information

Ardington – Wantage, Oxfordshire, OX12 8QA www.ardingtonhouse.com Tel 01235 821566 Contact for visiting information

Ascott House – Wing, Leighton Buzzard, Buckinghamshire, LU7 0PS www.ascottestate.co.uk or www.nationaltrust.org.uk Tel 01296 688242 Open late Mar–mid Sept, Tue–Sun & BH Mon (Tue–Thur & BH Mon in late Apr–late Jul) 2–6pm

Ashdown House – Lambourn, Newbury, Berkshire, RG17 8RE www.nationaltrust.org.uk Tel 01793 762209/01494 755569 Open Apr–Oct, Wed & Sat, 2–5pm

Ashridge – Ashridge Estate, Moneybury Hill, Ringshall, Berkhamsted, Hertfordshire, HP4 1LX www.nationaltrust.org.uk Tel 01442 851227/01494 755557 Estate open all year, daily 10am–5pm (For information on Ashridge College, contact 01442 843491)

Balliol College – Broad Street, Oxford, Oxfordshire, OX1 3BJ www.visitoxford.org & www.balliol.ox.ac.uk Tel 01865 277777 Open all year, daily 2–5pm

Bedford: Castle Close – Cecil Higgins Art Gallery, Castle Lane, Bedford, Bedfordshire, MK40 3RP www.cecilhigginsartgallery.org Tel 01234 211222 Closed for refurbishment at the time of writing

Bleinheim Palace – Woodstock, Oxfordshire, OX20 1PX www.blenheimpalace.com Tel 08700 602080 Open mid-Feb–mid-Dec, daily (Wed–Sun in Nov–mid-Dec) 10.30am–5.30pm

Bletchley Park – The Mansion, Bletchley Park, Bletchley, Milton Keynes, MK3 6EB www.bletchleypark.org.uk 01908 640404 Open all year, daily 9.30am–5pm (from 10.30am on Sat–Sun & BH in Apr–Oct, 10.30am–4pm in Nov–Mar)

Boarstall Tower – Boarstall, Aylesbury, Buckinghamshire, HP18 9UX www.nationaltrust.org.uk Tel 01280 822850 (Mon–Fri) Open only on specific days: contact for further information

Brasenose College – Radcliffe Square, Oxford, Oxfordshire, OX1 4AJ www.visitoxford.org & www.bnc.ox.ac.uk Tel 01865 277830 Open all year, daily 2–4pm (to groups 10–11.30am, and until 5pm in summer)

Brocket Hall Hotel – Welwyn, Hertfordshire, AL8 7XG www.brocket-hall.co.uk Tel 01707 335241

Broughton Castle – Broughton, Nr Banbury, Oxfordshire, OX15 5EB www.broughtoncastle.com Tel 01295 262624 Open Easter Sun & Mon, & early May–mid-Sep, Wed, Sun & BH Mon (plus Thur in Jul–Aug) 2–5pm; groups by appointment all year

Buscot Old Parsonage – Buscot, Faringdon, Oxfordshire, SN7 8DQ www.nationaltrust.org.uk Tel 01793 762209 Open Apr–Oct, Wed 2–6pm by written appointment with the tenant

Buscot Park – Buscot, Faringdon, Oxfordshire, SN7 8BU www.nationaltrust.org.uk Tel 0845 3453387/01367 240786 Open early Apr–late Sep, Wed–Fri & BH Mons (plus some weekends) 2–6pm

Bushmead Priory – Colmworth, Bedfordshire, MK44 2LD www.english-heritage.org.uk/bushmead Tel 01525 860000 Open May–Aug, on first Sat in month for pre-booked guided tours only

Chalfont St Giles: Milton's Cottage – Deanway, Chalfont St Giles, Buckinghamshire, HP8 4JH www.miltonscottage.org Tel 01494 872313 Open Mar–Oct, Tue–Sun & BH Mon 10am–1pm & 2–6pm

Chastleton House – Chastleton, Nr Moreton-in-Marsh, Oxfordshire, GL56 0SU www.nationaltrust.org.uk Tel 01608 674981/01494 755560 Open Apr–Oct, Wed–Sat 1–5pm (to 4pm in Oct) by pre-booked timed tickets only

Chenies Manor – Chenies, Buckinghamshire, WD3 6ER www.cheniesmanorhouse.co.uk Tel 01494 762888 Open early Apr–late Oct, Wed, Thur & BH Mon 2–5pm

Chiltern Open Air Museum – Newland Park, Gorelands Lane, Chalfont St. Giles, Buckinghamshire, HP8 4AB www.coam.org.uk Tel 01494 871117 Open Apr–Oct, daily 10am–5pm

Chilton House – Chilton, Aylesbury, Buckinghamshire, HP18 9LR www.chiltonhouse.co.uk Tel 01844 265200 Contact the house for visiting information

Christ Church College – St Aldates, Oxford, Oxfordshire, OX1 1DP www.visitoxford.org & www.chch.ox.ac.uk Tel 01865 286573 Open all year, daily 9am–5.30pm (from 1pm on Sun)

Claydon House – Middle Claydon, Buckinghamshire, MK18 2EY www.nationaltrust.org.uk Tel 01296 730349/01494 755561 Open early Mar–early Nov, Sat–Wed (& Good Fri) 1–5pm or dusk, if earlier

Cliveden – Cliveden House Hotel, Cliveden, Taplow, Berkshire, SL6 0JF www.clivedenhouse.co.uk Tel 01628 668561. Also: Cliveden House & Gardens, Cliveden, Taplow, Berkshire, SL6 0JA www.nationaltrust.org.uk Tel 01628 605069/01494 755562 Grounds open late Feb–late Dec, daily 11am–6pm (to 4pm in Nov–Dec); part of house open Apr–Oct, Thur & Sun 3–5.30pm (admission by timed ticket)

Cogges Manor – Cogges Manor Farm Museum, Church Lane, Witney, Oxfordshire, OX28 3LA www.cogges.org Tel 01993 772602 Open early Apr–late Aug, Tue–Sun 10.30am–5.30pm (from 11am on Sat, Sun & BH)

Corpus Christi College – Merton Street, Oxford, Oxfordshire, OX1 4JF www.visitoxford.org & www.ccc.ox.ac.uk Tel 01865 276700 Open all year, daily 1.30–4.30pm

Ditchley Park – Enstone, Oxfordshire, OX7 4ER www.ditchley.co.uk Tel 01608 677346 Open by arrangement only

Dorney Court – Dorney, Nr Windsor, Berkshire, SL4 6QP www.dorneycourt.co.uk Tel 01628 604638 Open May, BH Suns & Mons, & Aug, Sun–Fri; 1.30–4pm

Ewelme Almshouses – Parsons Lane, Ewelme, Oxfordshire, OX10 6HS The exterior of the almshouses is accessible to visitors all year

Exeter College – Turl Street, Oxford, Oxfordshire, OX1 3DP www.visitoxford.org & www.exeter.ox.ac.uk Tel 01865 279600 Open all year, daily 2–5pm

Fawley Court – Marlow Road, Henley-on-Thames, Oxfordshire, RG9 3AE In the process of being sold at the time of writing

Gorhambury – St Albans, Hertfordshire, AL3 6AH Tel 01727 854051 Open May–Sep, Thurs 2–5pm

Grey's Court – Rotherfield Greys, Henley-on-Thames, Oxfordshire, RG94 4PG www.nationaltrust.org.uk Tel 01491 628529/01494 755564 House closed until April 2010 for conservation work; gardens open early Apr–late Sep, Wed–Sun & BH Mon (closed Good Fri) 12–5pm

Hanbury Manor Hotel – Ware, Hertfordshire, SG12 0SD Tel 01920 487722

Hartwell House Hotel – Oxford Road, Nr Aylesbury, Buckinghamshire, HP17 8NR www.hartwell-house.com Tel 01296 747444

Hatfield House & Old Palace – Hatfield, Hertfordshire, AL9 5NQ www.hatfield-house.co.uk Tel 01707 287010 Open Easter–late Sep, Wed–Sun & BH Mon 12–5pm

Hertford College – Catte Street, Oxford, Oxfordshire, OX1 3BW www.visitoxford.org & www.hertford.ox.ac.uk Tel 01865 279400 Open all year, daily 10am–dusk (closed 12–2pm)

Houghton House – Hazelwood Lane, Ampthill, Bedfordshire, MK45 2EZ www.english-heritage.org.uk/houghton Tel 01223 582700 (regional office) Open all year, at any reasonable time

Hughenden Manor – High Wycombe, Buckinghamshire, HP14 4LA www.nationaltrust.org.uk Tel 01494 755573/755565 Open early Mar–late Oct, Wed–Sun & BH Mon 1–5pm

Jesus College – Turl Street, Oxford, Oxfordshire, OX1 3DW www.visitoxford.org & www.jesus.ox.ac.uk Tel 01865 279700 Open all year, daily 2–4.30pm

Keble College – Parks Road, Oxford, Oxfordshire, OX1 3PG www.visitoxford.org & www.keble.ox.ac.uk Tel 01865 272727 Open all year, daily 2–5pm

Kelmscott Manor – Kelmscott, Nr Lechdale, Gloucestershire, GL7 3HJ www.kelmscottmanor.co.uk Tel 01367 252486 Open Apr–Sep, Wed & every 1st and 3rd Sat 11am–5pm, by timed ticket; open to groups, booked in advance, Thur & Fri; gardens also open on Thurs 2–5pm in May–Jun

Kingston Bagpuize House – Abingdon, Oxfordshire, OX13 5AX www.kingstonbagpuizehouse.org.uk Tel 01865 820259 Open Feb–Sep, on certain days 2–5.30pm

Knebworth House – Knebworth, Hertfordshire, SG3 6PY www.knebworthhouse.com Tel 01438 812661 Open late Mar–late Sep, Sat–Sun & BHs (daily in school holidays) 12–5pm

Letchworth: 296 Norton Way South – First Garden City Heritage Museum, 296 Norton Way South, Letchworth Garden City, Hertfordshire, SG6 1SU www.letchworthgc.com Tel 01462 482710 Open all year, Mon–Sat 10am–5pm

Lincoln College – Turl Street, Oxford, Oxfordshire, OX1 3DR www.visitoxford.org & www.linc.ox.ac.uk Tel 01865 279800 Open all year, daily 2–5pm (from 11am on Sun)

Magdalen College – High Street, Oxford, Oxfordshire, OX1 4AU www.visitoxford.org & www.magd.ox.ac.uk Tel 01865 276000 Open all year, daily 1–6pm (from 12pm in Jul–Sep)

Mapledurham House – Mapledurham, Reading, Berkshire, RG4 7TR www.mapledurham.co.uk Tel 01189 723350 Open Easter–Sep, Sat–Sun & BHs 2–5.30pm

Merton College – Merton Street, Oxford, Oxfordshire, OX1 4JD www.visitoxford.org & www.merton.ox.ac.uk Tel 01865 276310 Open all year, daily 2–4pm (from 10am on Sat & Sun)

Milton Manor House – Milton, Abingdon, Oxfordshire, OX14 4EN www.miltonmanorhouse.com Tel 0845 6807130 Open Easter–Aug, BH Sun & Mon (also open daily during some weeks of Whitsun & summer holidays) 2–5pm

Minster Lovell Hall – Witney, Oxfordshire www.english-heritage.org.uk/minsterlovell Tel 01424 775705 Open all year, daily at any reasonable time

Moor Park – Rickmansworth, Hertfordshire, WD3 1QN www.moorparkgc.co.uk Tel 01923 773146 Contact the golf club for opening information

Nether Winchenden House – Nether Winchendon, Nr Aylesbury, Buckinghamshire, HP18 0DY www.netherwinchendonhouse.co.uk Tel 01844 290101 Open May (plus the Aug BH Mon), daily 2.30–5.30pm for tours

New College – New College Lane, Oxford, Oxfordshire, OX1 3BN www.visitoxford.org & www.new.ox.ac.uk Tel 01865 279555 Open all year, daily 11am–5pm (2–4pm in Oct–Easter)

Nuffield College – New Road, Oxford, Oxfordshire, OX1 1NF www.visitoxford.org & www.nuff.ox.ac.uk Tel 01865 278500 Open all year, daily 9am–5pm

Nuffield Place – Huntercombe, nr Nettlebed, Henley-on-Thames, Oxfordshire, RG9 5RY Closed at the time of writing. Contact the Friends of Nuffield Place: www.nuffield-place.com, tel 01494 641224

Nuneham Courtneay – Global Retreat Centre, Nuneham Park, Nuneham Courtenay, Oxfordshire, OX44 9PG www.globalretreatcentre.org.uk Tel 01865 343551 Contact the centre for visiting information

Old Warden Park & Swiss Cottage – Old Warden Park, Nr Biggleswade, Bedfordshire, SG18 9EP www.shuttleworthpark.co.uk Tel 01767 626200 Contact to arrange access to the house. Shuttleworth Collection & Swiss Cottage www.shuttleworth.org 01767 627927 Open all year, daily 9.30am–5pm (to 4pm in Nov–Mar)

Olney: Cowper's House – The Cowper and Newton Museum, Orchard Side, Market Place, Olney, Buckinghamshire, MK46 4AJ www.cowperandnewtonmuseum.org.uk Tel 01234 711516 Open early Mar–late Dec, Tue–Sat & BH Mons (closed Good Fri) 10.30am–4.30pm

Oriel College – Oriel Square, Oxford, Oxfordshire, OX1 4EW www.visitoxford.org & www.oriel.ox.ac.uk Tel 01865 276555 Open all year, daily 1–4pm

Pembroke College – St Aldates, Oxford, Oxfordshire, OX1 1DW www.visitoxford.org & www.pmb.ox.ac.uk Tel 01865 276444 Open by appointment only

The Queen's College – High Street, Oxford, Oxfordshire, OX1 4AW www.visitoxford.org & www.queens.ox.ac.uk Tel 01865 279120 Open by appointment only

Rousham Park – Nr Steeple Aston, Bicester, Oxfordshire, OX25 4QX www.rousham.org Tel 01869 347110 Open to groups by arrangement only; gardens open all year, daily 10am–4.30pm

St Catherine's College – Manor Road, Oxford, Oxfordshire, OX1 3UJ www.visitoxford.org & www.stcatz.ox.ac.uk Tel 01865 271700 Open all year, daily 9–5pm

St Edmund Hall – Queens Lane, Oxford, Oxfordshire, OX1 4AR www.visitoxford.org & www.seh.ox.ac.uk Tel 01865 279000 Open all year, daily during daylight hours

St John's College –St Giles, Oxford, Oxfordshire, OX1 3JP www.visitoxford.org & www.sjc.ox.ac.uk Tel 01865 277300 Open all year, daily 1–5pm or dusk, if earlier

Shaw's Corner – Ayot St Lawrence, Welwyn, Hertfordshire, AL6 9BX www.nationaltrust.org.uk Tel 01438 820307/01438 829221 Open mid-Mar–late Oct, Wed–Sun & BHs 1–5pm

Shipton-under-Wychwood: Shaven Crown – The Shaven Crown Hotel, High Street, Shipton-under-Wychwood, Oxfordshire, OX7 6BA www.theshavencrown.co.uk Tel 01993 830330

Stoke Park – Stoke Park Club, Park Road, Stoke Poges, Buckinghamshire, SL2 4PG www.stokeparkclub.com Tel 01753 717171

Stonor – Henley-on-Thames, Oxfordshire, RG9 6HF www.stonor.com Tel 01491 638587 Open early Apr–mid-Sep, Sun & BH Mon (also Wed in Jul–Aug) 2–5.30pm

Stowe House – Buckingham, Buckinghamshire, MK18 5EH. For information on open days at the school contact The Stowe House Preservation Trust, www.shpt.org, tel 01280 818166/818229. The gardens are run by The National Trust – see Gothic Temple below for details

Stowe Park: Gothic Temple – Stowe Landscape Gardens, Buckingham, Buckinghamshire, MK18 5DQ www.nationaltrust.org.uk Tel 01280 822850/01494 755568 Open all year, Wed–Sun 10.30am–5.30pm (Sat–Sun 10.30am–4pm in Nov–Feb)

Taplow Court – Berry Hill, Taplow, Nr Maidenhead, Berkshire, SL6 0ER www.sgi-uk.org Tel 01628 773163 Open Jun–Aug, 1st Sun in the month, 2–5.30pm

Trinity College – Broad Street, Oxford, Oxfordshire, OX1 3BH www.visitoxford.org & www.trinity.ox.ac.uk Tel 01865 279900 Open all year, 10am–12pm on Mon–Fri & 2–4pm daily (also 10am–12pm on Sat–Sun in college vacations)

University College – High Street, Oxford, Oxfordshire, OX1 4BH www.visitoxford.org & www.univ.ox.ac.uk Tel 01865 276602 Open by appointment only

Waddesdon Manor – Waddesdon, Nr Aylesbury, Buckinghamshire, HP18 0JH www.waddesdon.org.uk or www.nationaltrust.org.uk Tel 01296 653226/653211 Open Apr–Oct, Wed–Sun (Bachelor's Wing open Wed–Fri) 12–4pm (from 11am on Sat & Sun); also open for pre-Christmas season, contact for information

Wadham College – Parks Road, Oxford, Oxfordshire, OX1 3PN www.visitoxford.org & www.wadham.ox.ac.uk Tel 01865 277900 Open all year, daily 1–4.15pm (also 10.30–11.45am during college vacations)

West Wycombe Park – West Wycombe, Buckinghamshire, HP14 3AJ www.nationaltrust.org.uk Tel 01494 513569/755571 Open Jun–Aug, Sun–Thur 2–6pm (gardens also open from early Apr)

Weston Manor Hotel – Northampton Road, Weston-on-the-Green, Oxfordshire, OX25 3QL www.westonmanor.co.uk Tel 01869 350621

Woburn Abbey – Woburn, Bedfordshire, MK17 9WA www.discoverwoburn.co.uk Tel 01525 290333/292148 Open early Mar–early Oct, daily (Sat–Sun in Mar) 11am–4pm; park open all year, daily 10am–5pm (to 4.30pm in Oct–Mar)

Woodhall Park – Watton-at-Stone, Hertfordshire, SG14 3NG Tel 01920 830230 Open all year, at any reasonable time (preferably during school holidays) by prior arrangement

Worcester College – Worcester Street, Oxford, Oxfordshire, OX1 2HB www.visitoxford.org & www.worc.ox.ac.uk Tel 01865 278300 Open all year, daily 2–5pm

Wrest Park House & Pavilion – Silsoe, Bedfordshire, MK45 4HS www.english-heritage.org.uk/wrestpark Tel 01525 860152 Open Apr–Oct, Sat–Sun & BH Mon (Thurs–Mon in Jul–Aug) 10am–6pm (to 5pm in Oct)

Index

Main entries for houses are in **bold**

Discover Britain's Historic Houses: Middle England

Reader's Digest Project Team
Series editor Christine Noble
Project editor Lisa Thomas
Art editor Jane McKenna
Picture researcher Christine Hinze
Caption writer/copy editor Caroline Smith
Proofreader Ron Pankhurst
Indexer Marie Lorimer
Product production manager Claudette Bramble
Production controller Katherine Tibbals

Reader's Digest General Books
Editorial director Julian Browne
Art director Anne-Marie Bulat
Managing editor Nina Hathway
Picture resource manager Sarah Stewart-Richardson
Pre-press account manager Dean Russell

Colour origination Colour Systems Limited, London
Printed and bound in China

We are committed both to the quality of our products and the service we provide to our customers. We value your comments, so please do contact us on **08705 113366** or via our web site at **www.readersdigest.co.uk**
If you have any comments or suggestions about the content of our books, you can contact us at:
gbeditorial@readersdigest.co.uk

Published by The Reader's Digest Association Limited, 11 Westferry Circus, Canary Wharf, London E14 4HE

www.readersdigest.co.uk

This book was designed, edited and produced by The Reader's Digest Association Limited based on material from *England's Thousand Best Houses* by Simon Jenkins, first published by Allen Lane, the Penguin Press, a publishing division of Penguin Books Ltd.

Concept code UK0149/L/S
Book code 634-007 UP0000-2
ISBN 978 0 276 44310 7
Oracle code 356600007H.00.24